The Nitty-Gritty Classroom and Behavior Management Resource

Strategies, Reproducibles, and Tips for Teachers

Belinda Christine Tetteris

Rowman & Littlefield Education
Lanham, Maryland • Toronto • Oxford
2006

Published in the United States of America
by Rowman & Littlefield Education
A Division of Rowman & Littlefield Publishers, Inc.
A wholly owned subsidiary of The Rowman & Littlefield Publishing Group, Inc.
4501 Forbes Boulevard, Suite 200, Lanham, Maryland 20706
www.rowmaneducation.com

PO Box 317
Oxford
OX2 9RU, UK

British Library Cataloguing in Publication Information Available

Library of Congress Cataloging-in-Publication Data
Tetteris, Belinda Christine
   The nitty-gritty classroom and behavior management resource : strategies, reproducibles,
and tips for teachers / Belinda Christine Tetteris.
      p. cm.
   Includes bibliographical references and index.
   ISBN-13: 978-1-57886-497-3 (pbk. : alk. paper)
   ISBN-10: 1-57886-497-6 (pbk. : alk. paper)
      1. Classroom management–Handbooks, manuals, etc. 2. Behavior modification–
Handbooks, manuals, etc.
   LB3013 .T47 2006
   371.102/4 22   2006045511

This book is dedicated to all teachers
with hopes of making their job just a little bit easier so they may
continue to inspire the future by teaching for many years to come.

Contents

Chapter Three: *Planning Efficiently and Effectively*

Chapter Four: *Record Keeping Made Simple*

Chapter Five: *Substitute Plans in a Snap*

Chapter Eight: *Home–School Connection Ideas*

Chapter Nine: *Methods for Teaching Reading Groups and Managing Centers*

Chapter Ten: *Helpful Hints about the Hidden Curriculum*

Chapter Eleven: *Useful Graphic Organizers*

Acknowledgments

♥ My husband, Anthony Tetteris, and my daughter, Brooke Tetteris, for supporting me as I fulfilled my dream of writing my book.

♥ My parents, Manilious and Marguerite Bolton, for providing me with the encouragement needed to become an educator.

♥ Melissa Lingenfelder, a wonderful friend and elementary school teacher that I have had long discussions with on inspiring teaching ideas, what good instruction should look like, and dealing with teacher-related frustrations.

♥ Brittany Young, an aspiring teacher, who read and critiqued my book to make sure the reference material offered would also meet the needs of a new teacher.

♥ My colleagues, Michele Paris and Pat Hundley, for motivating me to publish my work.

♥ Principal Bob Findley, who has trusted my judgment as a professional educator and given me the liberty to teach using methods that I believe are appropriate for the needs of my students.

♥ And, finally, PR Graphics, Timonium, MD, for their assistance in the layout and design of my book.

Preface

Teachers convey the same message of feeling overwhelmed by the many high expectations of teaching. *The Nitty-Gritty Classroom and Behavior Management Resource* is designed to help conquer teacher-related frustrations by providing insight on practical techniques and tips used by effective teachers. This resource addresses topics such as innovative ideas for designing your classroom layout, establishing centers, effective planning tips, varieties of assessments, record-keeping techniques, useful behavior management strategies, helpful hints for establishing a positive home–school connection, differentiation ideas, methods for teaching reading groups and managing centers, and exciting ways to integrate the hidden curriculum.

This resource has been written by a master teacher who understands the challenges facing today's educators and has provided this reference to help teachers meet the professional challenges they are faced with every day.

The mission of this book is to help teachers better relate to, understand, and love their job by providing a practical professional resource that contains innovative ideas, visuals, and reproducibles that can be referenced quickly to help make the job of a teacher easier. If this book succeeds in helping even one teacher feel less overwhelmed and more successful, then it was well worth the time and effort. Best wishes!

Chapter 1
Classroom Set Up Made Easy

Summer break is over too soon of course and it is hard to believe that you are already jingling and fumbling around with the keys to your classroom. You open the door and look around at the bare walls, empty chalkboards, stacked chairs, and clean desks. Ideas about how you want the classroom to look are swirling around in your mind. Chapter one will focus on the classroom set up made easy by helping you to plan your classroom components, select a seating arrangement, draw a diagram of your classroom layout, and set up furniture and learning aids in your room efficiently.

Classroom Components

Always use brain before brawn when setting up a classroom. Before you begin to move desks and tables you should read this chapter in its entirety so that you will be better able to make a list of components you wish to include in your classroom. This classroom components list will serve as a reference when designing a diagram of your ideal classroom layout.

If this is your first year as a classroom teacher or if you have transferred to a new school then visit with colleagues on your grade level and they can inform you of essential components that are expected to be included in your classroom. You should be aware that some principals require each departmentalized grade level to maintain identical classroom set ups which would allow students that move from room to room to be familiar with where to find the learning resources. Other principals allow the classroom teacher to select their own classroom set up based on their student's needs. It is important that you are informed of these requirements before you begin to plan your classroom layout. Your elementary classroom components list may contain the following:

Classroom Components List:

❏ Teacher's Desk Area

❏ Calendar/Carpet Area

❏ Classroom Library

❏ Guided Reading Group Area

❏ Centers

❏ Student Desk Area

❏ Daily Schedule

❏ Daily Objectives

❏ Class Behavior Chart

❏ Class Job Assignments

❏ Word or Vocabulary Wall

❏ Sign Out Station/Hall Passes

❏ Alphabet and Number Line

❏ Color and Number Words Poster

❏ Writing/Editing Marks Poster

❏ Reading Strategies Poster

❏ Name Tags (Desks and Lockers/Cubbies)

Teacher's Desk Area

Desk? What desk? Most teachers use their desk as a dumping ground for their important paperwork and do most of their planning at the much larger reading group table. Since the teacher's desk does not play an important role in the teaching you will do on a day-to-day basis, put it to the side… literally. Place your desk in an area that won't be in the way of learning activities and teacher or student movement. The teacher's desk area must be strictly off limits to students since this is the place you will store your plan book, grade book, personal information, and notices from the office. ★**Tip:** You may want to consider using masking tape to create a Do Not Enter zone or perimeter on the floor around your desk as a visual for students to keep out. Now let's organize your dumping ground, or as you refer to it—your desk.

- Purchase a corkboard. A teacher always has important tasks and office paperwork that must be completed, so to make sure nothing is forgotten, hang a corkboard on the wall by your desk so you can thumbtack these important papers in a spot where they can be seen and remembered. For those of you who are extreme organizers you could label pocket folders and staple them to your corkboard in order to house your paperwork neatly at the same time affording you the ability to see what has been completed and what still needs to be done. Labeling ideas for corkboard pocket folder organizers:

– Absentee Notes/Late Slips	– Office Paperwork	– Student Referral Forms
– Meetings	– Parent Notes	– Urgent

- Connect your computer and practice accessing your professional e-mail. Also find out the location of the printer which your computer will print from.

- Establish an organization system for your desk top and drawers such as pencil holders, paper trays, bookends to contain your curriculum guides, and random baskets for separating supplies.

- Visit your school's supply closet or if necessary purchase the following materials and store them in your desk:

Professional Supplies

– dictionary	– thesaurus	– pens	– pencils
– color markers	– scented markers	– dry erase markers	– ruler
– overhead markers	– scissors	– correction fluid	– ink pad
– good work stamps	– stickers	– spiral notebook	– camera
– thumb tacks	– sticky notes	– paper clips	– glue
– chalkboard eraser	– chalk/color chalk	– stapler/staples	– magnets
– hot glue gun/glue sticks	– transparent tape	– masking tape	– a whistle
– key chain	– index cards	– screwdriver	– hole punch

Personal Supplies

– brush	– mirror	– lotion	– lip balm
– stash of candy	– nail file/clippers	– change for snacks	– a sweater
– clothes hangers	– slippers	– scarf/gloves	– sunglasses

- Place a calendar in a visible area to record and reference dates reserved for meetings, school closings, and special events.

- Purchase a paper tray for filing student papers that can be placed next to your desk for students to turn in class work, homework, and important information (permission slips, completed office forms, etc.). Label each tray as to what type of papers it will contain.

- Keep a file cabinet next to your desk. Filing activities and important papers will make teaching easier each year. Follow these steps to begin your filing system:

  — In the first and, if needed, the second, file cabinet drawer place one hanging file folder labeled for each subject that you teach.

  — Within the hanging file folders labeled for each subject, insert tabbed manila folders labeled for each unit of study within that subject. File each activity on a daily basis according to its subject and unit. Be sure to place all activities inside the manila folders in the order as to which they were taught. If any activity needs to be revised, make the necessary changes before filing for next year's use.

  — In the next available drawer hang file folders and insert labeled manila folders for each of the following topics:
    - Long Range Plans
    - Substitute Plans
    - Newsletters
    - Grade Level Meetings
    - Plans for the First Week of School
    - Holiday Activities
    - Report Cards
    - Conferences
    - Field Trips
    - Homework
    - Student Information
    - Parent Contact Information
    - Emergency Closing Information
    - IEP (Individualized Education Program) Information
    - Student Portfolios
    - Back-to-School Night or Open House
    - Committee Information
    - Observations
    - Absentee Notes
    - Student Referrals
    - Blank Behavior Charts
    - Teacher Workshop Information
    - Miscellaneous

Calendar/Carpet Area

The calendar or carpet area is very functional and versatile, making it an important part of your classroom layout. Students sit on the carpet to listen to shared readings, to hold group discussions, to watch the teacher model an objective, and to complete student interactive calendar activities. Since the carpet area is the place for calendar activities, its set up should be in front of a bulletin board. Sample calendar activities are shown below. In classrooms that lack space, the carpet area is also where the teacher and students sit on the floor and conduct guided reading groups. Teachers can maximize this space by placing a bookshelf on one side of the carpet to create a classroom library.

The calendar or carpet area is most commonly found in pre-kindergarten through second grade. Third through fifth grades may maintain a calendar/carpet area, however, the calendar information is updated daily by a student (not the entire group) and the carpet is optional and often placed in the calendar area when it doubles as a class library. To design a calendar/carpet area in your room you may need:

- A bulletin board or empty wall area to place calendar activities.

- Calendar activities appropriate for your grade level such as a calendar, the date written out on a laminated sentence strip, months of the year, a weather chart, a pattern activity, a counting and tracking system to record how many days students have been in school, a counting money activity, counting using a hundreds chart, a poem of the month, and any other relevant interactive curriculum activity that you would like to add. Refer to chapter ten for more information on calendar activities.

- A carpet large enough for all of your students to be able to sit and fit on.

- One adult-size rocking chair and a wipe board/easel (optional for intermediate).

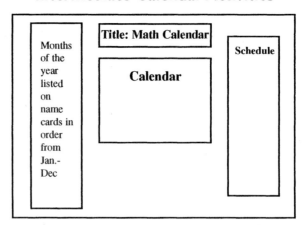

Primary Calendar Activities

Months of the year listed on name cards in order from Jan - Dec	Title: Math Calendar	100's Chart
	Calendar	
	Today is (Month) (Day), (Year)	
	How many days have we been in school? Hundreds, Tens, Ones	Weather Wheel

Intermediate Calendar Activities

| Months of the year listed on name cards in order from Jan.- Dec | Title: Math Calendar | Schedule |
| | **Calendar** | |

Calendar activities can be completed as a morning activity or as a warm-up activity before math instruction. Calendar activities may vary according to grade level. Refer to your math curriculum guide or visit other classrooms within your grade level to acquire age-appropriate calendar ideas.

Classroom Library

Establishing a classroom library is an essential component for all classrooms. A classroom library will provide students with access to current reading materials which have been organized according to themes or topics. Building and maintaining a class library can be as easy as 1-2-3, just follow these easy steps for classroom library success:

1. Build your classroom library.
   - New books are expensive and it is very disappointing to see books frequently destroyed by student misuse or overuse. Instead of purchasing new books, go to your local public library, thrift stores, flea markets, and yard sales to buy used children's books for under a dollar or two.
   - Ask parents to donate appropriate books for the class library.
   - Purchase a variety of books that are age and curriculum appropriate, up to date, and multicultural.

2. Organize your classroom library with *book bins* (plastic buckets large enough to contain a group of similar books), labeled themes, and color dot stickers for coding books.
   - Sort the books into several different themes such as genres, authors, and topics.
   - Purchase plastic bins to organize and group the books according to how you have sorted them. Now your library books can be organized within book bins.
   - Label each book bin according to its theme (Fiction, Non-Fiction, Mystery, People, Places, Math, School, Science, Picture Books, Chapter Books). Primary grades should provide picture clues for each book bin label.
   - Use color dot stickers to code books so that each book is always placed in its correct book bin. For each theme, place matching color coded dot stickers on the right-hand corner of each book and book bin label (the fiction book bin label and books have matching blue stickers, the non-fiction book bin label and books have matching red stickers, etc.).

3. Maintain an organized library.
   - Teach the students how to use the classroom library's organization system. Emphasize the importance of student responsibility and ownership of the class library.
   - Assign a different student to be the classroom librarian each week. The librarian will check the books at the end of the day to make sure they have been put back correctly and neatly.

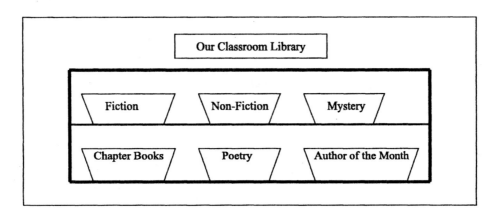

Guided Reading Group Area

Include a guided reading area in your classroom set up since reading is a vital part of the curriculum which must be taught on a daily basis. Guided reading groups occur when the teacher directly instructs small groups of students on their instructional reading level to help them become independent readers. During guided reading, students utilize their reading strategies to decode text, work on their fluency, read with voice inflection, analyze illustrations, discuss text features, and demonstrate comprehension skills. When ready, refer to chapter nine for information regarding how to teach guided reading groups, but for now focus on setting up the area.

Most reading groups congregate at a kidney- or rainbow-shaped reading table. Principals are usually accommodating when teachers request the purchase of the kidney table. If a new table is not in your school's budget, then resort to creating your own reading table by placing two rectangular tables together in the form of an L.

The guided reading table can also be a great place to conduct teacher-student conferences, parent-teacher conferences, and mini re-teaching lessons to support struggling students in other academic areas. When setting up your reading group area, implement the following:

- Choose a location for your reading group area that allows you to simultaneously teach reading and oversee all other student activities such as centers and seatwork.

- Set up the reading group table near a chalkboard or have a portable wipe board available for demonstrating teaching points during your reading lessons.

- Reading strategies should be posted on a wall near the reading area for students to reference. Colleagues will be able to provide you with the universal reading strategies that are used in your school, or refer to chapter nine for reading strategy cues.

- Hang a pocket chart where it can be easily accessed for displaying and discussing new vocabulary words.

- Place a small bookshelf with baskets (for organization) near your reading table for storing books, stickers, sticky notes, bookmarks, pointers, dry erase boards and markers, pencils, erasers, paper, glue sticks, scissors, and other teaching tools.

- Purchase the following teaching tools to motivate your students during reading:
  - Monster fingers (Halloween merchandise) for students to wear on their pointer finger or plastic decorative drink stirs to point with while tracking words. Fluent readers could use bookmarks to guide them while keeping their place as they read.
  - Colorful index cards with a small rectangular hole cut from the center of each card for finding and framing vocabulary words within the text (referred to as Going on a Word Hunt).
  - Headphones that no longer work (be sure to cut off the cord) for students to wear and block out distractions as they read.
  - Phonics phones (connect two pieces of $1\frac{1}{2}$ elbow PVC pipe in order to make a phone) for students to hear themselves as they read.
  - Sticky notes for highlighting and discussing important parts of the text.

Centers

It is too early to create centers related to the curriculum and student needs but the following four staple centers can be set up in order to get you started. The class library, writing, listening, and computer centers are referred to as *staple centers* because they are commonly used year round by changing the activity as necessary. As you begin teaching reading groups and getting to know the students, you can start introducing more centers around your classroom. Refer to chapter nine for detailed information on teaching reading groups, center ideas, and ways to manage centers.

- *Classroom Library:* This is a quiet reading area in the primary and intermediate classroom where students have access to current reading materials which have been organized for easy access according to themes or topics. Students can choose to read books quietly to themselves, stuffed animals, or a buddy. Other activities could include making bookmarks, publishing books, and demonstrating comprehension skills by writing and drawing about a story they have read. ★**Tip:** Post a map of the world on the wall next to the library for students to find the places they are reading about. Organization for this center is mentioned earlier in this chapter.

- *Writing Center:* Students are able to create, explore, and extend their writing abilities by using pens, pencils, markers, crayons, mini chalkboards, chalk, stationery, lined paper, envelopes, index cards, construction paper, stamps, stickers, stencils, writing prompts, and children's dictionaries. This center is appropriate for primary and intermediate grades. To create this center set up two desks side by side and place a tablecloth over both tabletops. Contain materials for this center using an organization system with drawers that are labeled as to which supply it contains. To enhance your writing center add a mailbox for students to exchange letters with fellow classmates.

- *Listening Center:* The listening center is an exciting center to include in any classroom from the primary to the intermediate grades. This center will help shape students into proficient oral readers and also help to develop their comprehension skills as they listen to pre-recorded tapes which have been purchased or recorded by fellow students or the teacher. To create this center you may choose to set up a tent with lots of windows (to be able to monitor student listening activities happening inside the tent), or establish a cozy corner with a plastic crate turned upside down to serve as a table for the tape player and large pillows for seats. Another idea is to simply place two desks next to each other with the tape player placed on the desktop for students to sit at and enjoy stories. Provide pencils, clipboards, blank paper for student reflections, and an activity related to the story on tape for students to complete. Other books on tape should be available for early finishers. ★**Tip:** Primary teachers should place a green dot sticker on the tape player's play button, a red dot sticker on the stop button, and a yellow dot sticker on the rewind button to help students become independent as they use the tape player functions.

- *Computer Center:* All primary and intermediate classrooms in this day and age should have an area designated to providing students with exposure to technology. Computers in the classroom are necessary for student practice with manipulating the mouse and cursor, keyboarding skills, and navigating the Internet. Be sure to provide headphones for each computer to eliminate noise distractions. It is very important that you choose computer software that has been approved by your school district. Check with your school's librarian or technology liaison in order to receive a list of approved computer software.

Seating Arrangements

Consider how you will facilitate student learning when deciding on the type of desk arrangement that will be established for your classroom layout. With any seating arrangement you choose it is imperative that every student can easily view your schedule, chalkboard, word walls, and any other boards that are important to the student's learning success. Once your seats have been arranged, check to see that you can physically get to each desk effortlessly in order to assist students. The following seating arrangements promote close proximity between teacher and students by providing pathways for teacher circulation.

- Cluster Arrangements

    Will your teaching style and lesson plans incorporate cooperative learning? If you plan to have your students working in cooperative groups (students working together to achieve a common goal) then consider a cluster arrangement. See figure 1.1 and figure 1.2 for cluster arrangement examples.

Figure 1.1

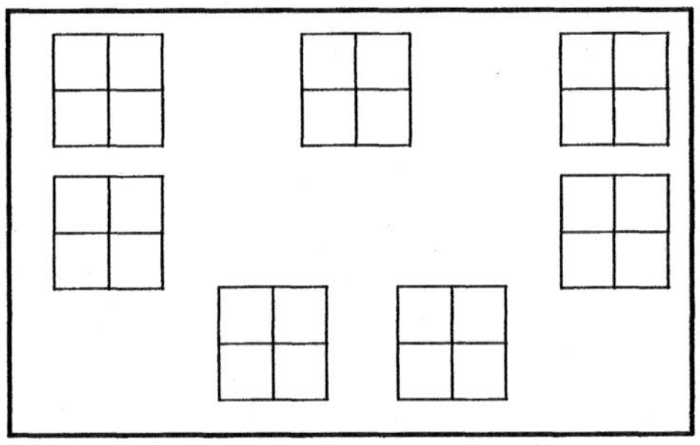

Figure 1.2

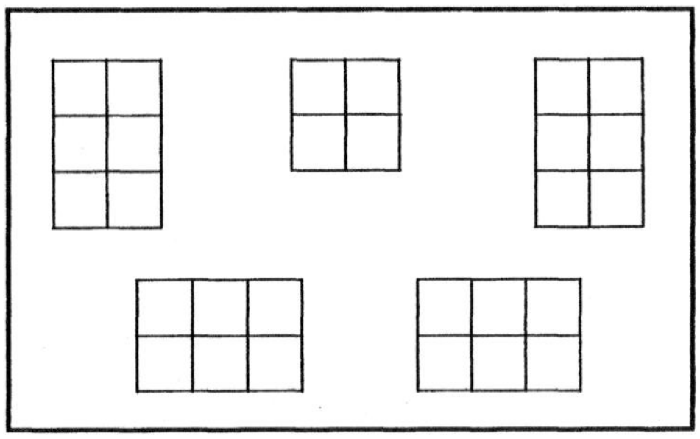

- The Inverted E

    If you plan to have your students work independently and with partners then you may want to consider establishing the inverted E (see figure 1.3).

Figure 1.3

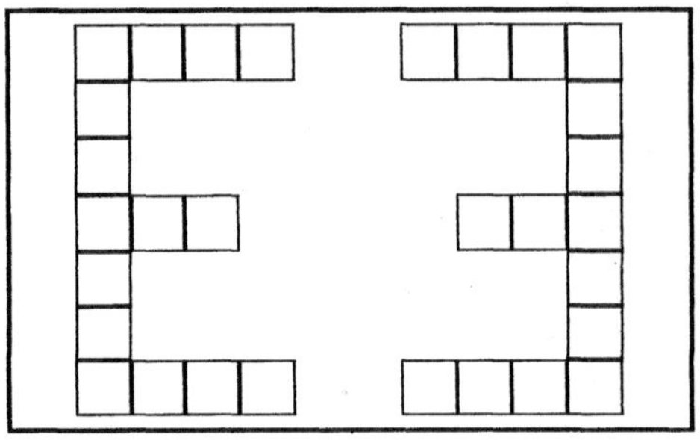

- Open Area Configuration

  The open area configuration is ideal for conducting class discussions (see figure 1.4). This arrangement also allows students to work independently or with partners. Utilizing the open area configuration gives the teacher the benefit of a work area in the center of the desks. The work area could be used for the placement of an overhead or teacher demonstrations.

Figure 1.4

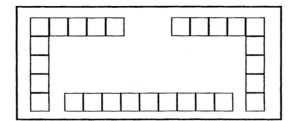

- Desk arrangements are not limited to the examples given. Any seating arrangement that creates a cooperative learning community and offers teacher mobility to access all students is acceptable.

- Desk isolation is the only arrangement that you want to avoid. Teachers need to provide opportunities for students to communicate and collaborate through sharing ideas, sharing responsibilities, and peer teaching so they are better able to achieve these social skills as they become adults in the working world.

- Experiment with different desk arrangements to find the seating arrangement that works best with your teaching style.

Name Tags

- Desk name tags can be purchased from teacher supply stores and come in different varieties with references printed on the tag such as the alphabet, number line, color words, number words, hundreds chart, multiplication chart, etc. Another choice is to simply write each student's name on a sentence strip and laminate it. Choose a name tag that is age appropriate and suits the needs of your students. Secure desk name tags by laminating and applying Velcro to the back of the tag and the desktop so that it is removable or make the name tag stationary by securing it with clear packing tape.

- Name tags for lockers or cubbies can also be made by writing and laminating each student's name on a sentence strip or by printing their names on pages of themed note pads that come in many different shapes and fun pictures such as stars, buses, bugs, etc. Secure locker name tags with magnets or by tying yarn through the locker vents and a hole made through the name tag.

The Daily Schedule

A daily schedule should always be posted so that students, parents, principals, and the teacher can be aware of the routine for the day. Since the schedule is an important part of your classroom, it can be placed on its own bulletin board or in a pocket chart off to the side of the chalkboard. The following are tips for creating a daily schedule:

- A schedule is best displayed in a small pocket chart (because it is interchangeable) with sentence strips that list the times and activities planned for the day.

- Primary teachers may choose to provide picture clues to help students understand the schedule, which could be drawn, printed from a clip art program, or cut out from teacher product or advertisement magazines. Picture clue ideas are:

— Morning Work: picture of a sunshine or composition notebook

— Reading: picture of students reading books together at a reading table

— Math: picture of math manipulatives or random numbers

— Writing: picture of a pencil

— Phonics: picture of random alphabet letters

— Science: picture of seeds and a plant

— Social Studies: picture of a map or historical figures

— Independent Reading Time: picture of a student reading independently

— Quiet Time: picture of a cot with a student resting on it

— Art: picture of a paint brush and paint bottle

— Gym: picture of students playing in a sport-related activity

— Music: picture of a music note or musical instruments

— Library: picture of an assortment of books

— Lunch: picture of a lunch box

— Recess: picture of a playground

— Dismissal: picture of a book bag and/or a bus

The Daily Class Schedule	
9:15	Morning Work
9:30	Shared Reading
10:00	Guided Reading Groups
11:00	Independent Reading
11:10	Phonics
11:40	Lunch
12:10	Math
1:00	Recess
1:30	Science
2:00	Specials
2:45	Writing
3:20 Pack Up	3:30 Dismissal

Daily Objectives

Objectives explain what the students will be learning for the day and should be placed at the front of the room in an area that can be seen by all students. The chalkboard is the best place to display your objectives. Sometimes finding space on your chalkboard can be an issue. Follow these steps to make an objective display that will maximize your chalkboard space:

1. Laminate two color sentence strips together, one directly above the other. Leave a quarter inch of lamination around the perimeter of the sentence strips when cutting the extra lamination off.

2. Place strong magnets on the back of the laminated sentence strips so that they can be displayed on your chalkboard.

3. Do the same to create as many color coded objective strips as you will need for each subject that you will teach.

4. A sign for each subject that you will teach should be created, laminated, magnetized, and placed above each objective sentence strip that you display.

5. Use an overhead pen to write your objectives on the laminated objective sentence strip.

6. To erase the objective, simply run your objective sentence strip under water and dry with a paper towel.

Figure 1.5
Daily Objectives
Chalkboard Display

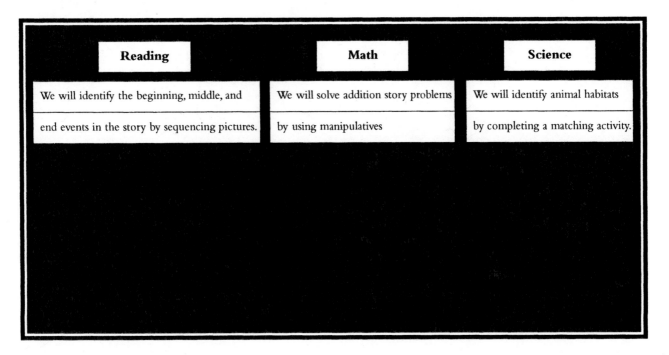

Class Behavior Chart

Learning will not occur in a classroom unless students feel safe and class activities are orderly. To establish a safe working environment, refer to chapter seven on behavior management, but for the purpose of just getting your behavior management started as part of your classroom layout follow the directions below.

The behavior chart below is for example purposes; see chapter seven for more class behavior chart ideas. The object of the behavior card chart is to have students move their name card each time they are not following the rules. The first time a student moves their card it goes under the sentence strip that states: I am following some of the rules. The second time a student moves their card it goes under the sentence strip that states: I am not following the rules. Each time a student moves their card they receive a consequence.

1. Place a large pocket chart at the front of the room and in the top pocket insert a sentence strip with the title *Class Behavior Chart*.

2. In the second pocket down, place a sentence strip stating: I am following the rules.

3. Within the third and fourth pocket on the pocket chart, place the index cards in a vertical position bearing each of the student's names.

4. For the fifth pocket down, place a sentence strip that states: I am following some of the rules.

5. In the eighth pocket down, place a sentence strip that states: I am not following the rules.

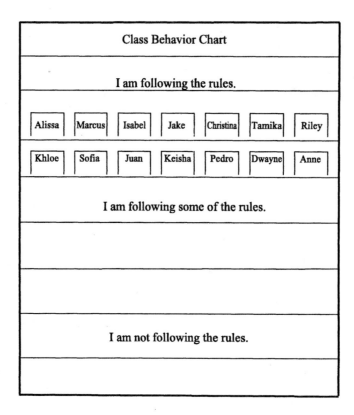

- Next to the behavior chart provide a list of consequences that will occur each time a student chooses not to follow the rules.

Consequences

I am following the rules:

Demonstrating Good Behavior

I am following some of the rules:

Verbal Warning

I am not following the rules:

Loss of 10 minutes from recess and
a note sent home.

- After your class has worked together to compose the classroom rules (as described in chapter seven) display them beside the class behavior chart.

Our Class Rules

1. We will be respectful.

2. We will raise our hand to speak.

3. We will listen to the speaker.

4. We will complete our work on time.

5. We will always do our best.

Class Job Chart or Helping Hands Chart

Students want to help out around the classroom because it makes them feel significant and it provides them with a sense of classroom ownership. To make a class job chart, do the following:

1. Choose an area to display a class jobs pocket chart.

2. Write job assignments on sentence strips and insert them into the pocket chart.
   Classroom jobs could consist of the following:
   — Plant Care Taker
   — Care Giver (takes care of the class pet)
   — Class Librarian (cleans and organizes the library)
   — Line Leader
   — Line Caboose
   — Messenger
   — Floor Monitor (sweeps and/or checks for clean floors)
   — Recess Helper (carries and collects recess equipment)
   — Hall Monitor (writes names of students who talk while walking in line)
   — Homework Helper (collects or checks homework)
   — Teacher Assistant (passes out activity sheets and graded assignments)
   — Lights (in charge of turning on and off the light when directed by teacher)
   — Door (in charge of holding/closing doors daily and during fire drills)
   — Calendar Helper (assists calendar activities)
   — Chalkboard (erases and cleans the board with a wet sponge)
   — Erasers (claps chalk dust out of chalkboard erasers)

3. Create student name cards on sentence strips or cut name tags in the shape of a hand (which can be created by the teacher with a die-cut machine or students can trace their hands and then write their name in the middle) and laminate them.

4. In order to assign jobs, place the selected student's name card next to the sentence strip that describes their job assignment. Job assignments should be rotated among groups of students each week to give everyone a fair turn.

HELPING HANDS JOB CHART	
Messenger	Jada
Homework Helper	Pedro
Teacher Assistant	Sofia
Recess Helper	Jevonte
Line Leader	Isabel

Starting the Word Wall

Primary classrooms usually provide a word wall for students to refer to as a spelling resource. Depending on the school's focus or departmentalization, intermediate classrooms may provide a vocabulary wall in place of a word wall which lists essential vocabulary words from math, science, or social studies units. Refer to chapter two on bulletin board displays for more in-depth information on word wall design options and uses, but for the sake of starting a word wall follow these guidelines:

● Create a title for the word wall or vocabulary wall (Our Class Word Wall or Our Math Words).

● Place the letters of the alphabet in alphabetical order, in rows, and with adequate space between and below each letter for mounting words (refer to chapter two for letter and word design ideas).

● It is too early to add vocabulary words to the word wall since they can only be added once the students learn them. Primary teachers, however, can display the students' names on the word wall by placing them under the alphabet letter that matches the letter the student's name begins with. The intermediate vocabulary wall should be designed but contain no words yet.

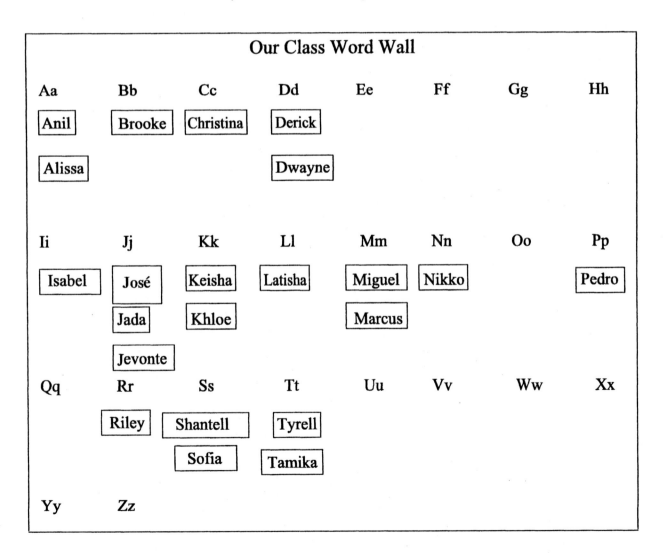

Sign-Out System

All classroom teachers must establish a class routine and monitoring system for students who leave the classroom to go to the office, nurse, and the bathroom. To monitor students as they leave the room, set up the following:

- A sign-out sheet that includes an area for students to write their name and the times they leave and return to the classroom.

- Clip this sign-out sheet to a clipboard. Secure the clipboard to a hook on the wall next to your classroom door.

- Fasten a pen to the clipboard by using a string of yarn with one end tied to the clip on the clipboard and the other end tied to the pen.

- Purchase a digital wristwatch and fasten it through the eye of the clipboard so students know the exact time to record as they leave and return to class.

- Next to the sign-out sheet, hang the hall passes. Hall passes can be purchased or created by the teacher and secured to the wall with adhesive hooks. Passes could be labeled as:

  — Hall pass

  — Bathroom pass

  — Office pass

  — Nurse pass

  — Library pass

Designing the Classroom Layout

After you have made a list of your necessary classroom components and decided on a seating arrangement, refer to these items in order to sketch a diagram of the classroom layout that you are envisioning. See diagram examples (figures 1.6). The classroom diagram can be drawn freehand or generated through the use of computer graphics. Your diagram will prove to be very helpful when setting up your room at the beginning of each academic year.

When designing a classroom layout keep in mind that a busy room can be a distraction for students. A classroom should be sterile for learning. When referring to the classroom environment, the word sterile means free from clutter, unnecessary posters, and furniture. Children with attention issues are more likely to concentrate and better process information within a sterile classroom environment so only post and include what is necessary.

Figure 1.6a
Sample Classroom Layout for Pre-Kindergarten and Kindergarten

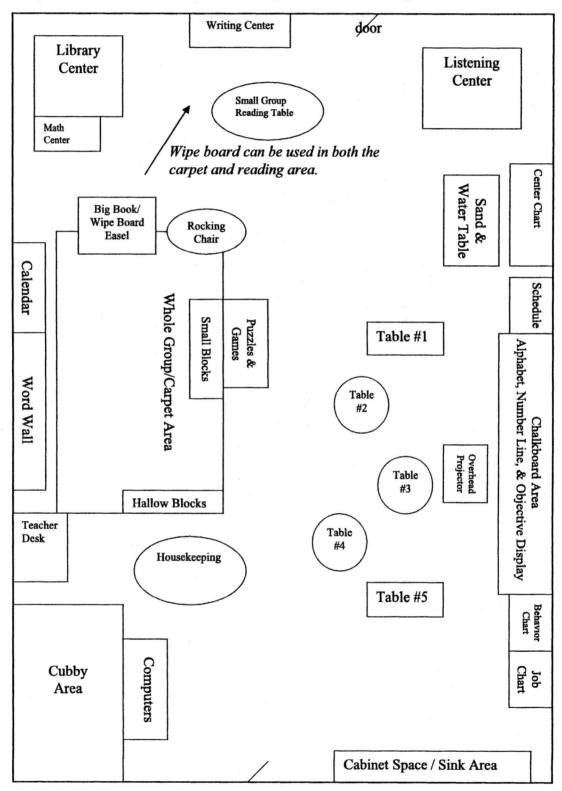

Figure 1.6b
Sample Classroom Layout for First and Second Grade

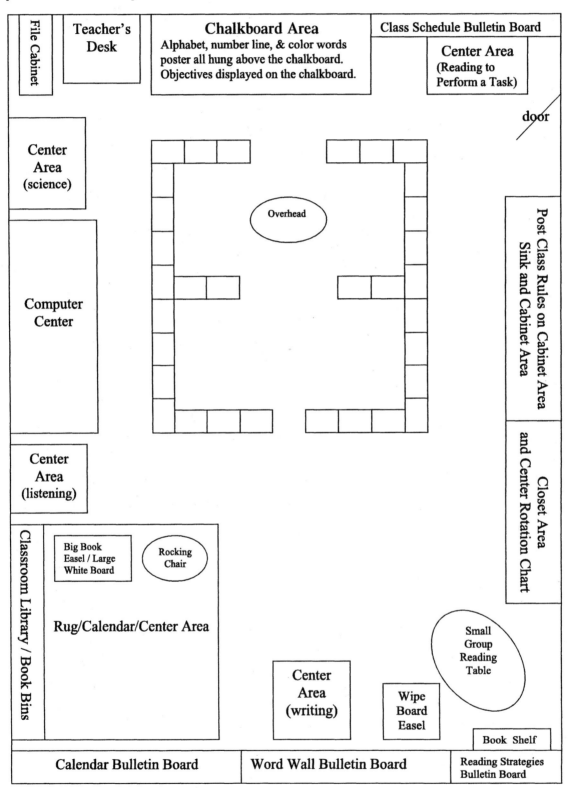

Figure 1.6c
Sample Classroom Layout for Third through Fifth Grade

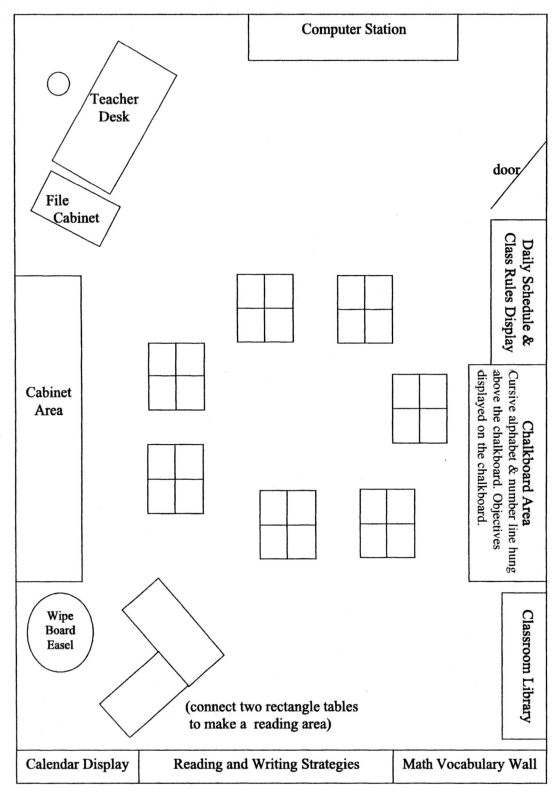

Chapter 2
Quick and Easy Bulletin Board Displays

Bulletin boards help make the classroom environment inviting for students and parents, however between planning, grading, conferences, meetings, committees, paperwork, and returning parent phone calls (phew!) there isn't much time left for coming up with creative bulletin board display ideas. To help lighten your planning load this chapter will provide you with bulletin board display tips and clever ideas to pick and choose from.

There are three options when deciding on the type of bulletin board display that you will utilize in the classroom: the informational bulletin board, the generic bulletin board, and the interactive bulletin board. Deciding on which bulletin board you will choose will depend on the time you plan to spend creating and changing displays throughout the year.

Creative Bulletin Board Materials

Clever ideas and eclectic materials help to make bulletin board displays interesting. From the background to the border, just use your imagination and have fun. Here are a few ideas to get the creativity juices flowing:

- Decide on a cohesive theme to display throughout your bulletin boards and classroom such as stars, rainbows, frogs, bugs, handprints, smiley faces, jungle or zoo animals, and primary colors.

- Use your choice of wallpaper, fabric, or colorful burlap when giving your bulletin board an interesting background. Bulletin board paper fades quickly and unless the paper is changed frequently it leaves displays looking unattractive. Wallpaper, fabric, and burlap can last for years without fading or ripping and it is much easier to hang and work with than bulletin board paper.

- Create an eye-catching border for your bulletin board by purchasing it from a teacher's supply store or by creating it yourself. Borders can be created by using wallpaper border, ribbon, die-cut shapes, or sentence strips that have been decorated by the teacher or students with glitter, marker, or paint.

- Bulletin boards should have a title for what you plan to display. Laminate your title so that it is reusable year after year. Words for the title could be made by writing on sentence strips, printing a banner with fun fonts from your word processor, painting on a large piece of paper, or using a die-cut machine to punch out letters using construction paper or wallpaper.

- Incorporating art work for your bulletin board's theme doesn't have to be a source of frustration. If you are not an *artist*, simply copy clip art onto a transparency and with an overhead projector display the transparency onto a large piece of tag board or construction paper, trace it, color it, and then laminate your finished piece. Another clever idea is to use placemats with related pictures to your display's theme. Placemats are cheap in price, vivid in color, and will last for many years to come.

● All students should be represented when displaying student work. Never display student work that has been graded or that bears grammatical errors.

Informational Bulletin Boards

Most classrooms boast informational bulletin boards that are displayed year round and require little or no updating, which ultimately conserves the teacher's time. Examples of informational bulletin board displays are:

● Reading Strategies:

Some classrooms emphasize the reading strategies by displaying them on a bulletin board near your reading group area. Most teachers choose to create a bulletin board near the reading table that displays the reading strategies because they are referred to on a daily basis before students begin reading and during guided reading group instruction. Inquire with a colleague about the universal reading strategies used in your school. If your school has not established reading strategies then refer to chapter nine for examples.

● Classroom News:

Design a classroom information bulletin board that is as close to the hallway as possible (so that it is accessible for parents) and that displays the class newsletter, volunteer information, homework assignments, dates of assemblies, field trip notices, school closings, early dismissal dates, report card distribution dates, conference schedules, class picture information, a monthly lunch menu, volunteer sign-up sheet (with a pen handy), and important schoolwide information. Update the posted information as necessary.

● Star Students:

Create a feeling of unity among your students with a bulletin board that displays everyone in the class by taking snapshot pictures of the students and labeling each picture with their names (either written by the student or teacher).

● Keeping Track:

Use a bulletin board to display a grid poster which could be used to track student progress in a variety of ways, such as students that complete their homework, monitoring how many books students read, rewarding good behavior, and recording when students reach their academic goals that have been set.

● Our _____ Grade Mission Statement:

Make a bulletin board that displays your class mission statement and let all the students sign it with a marker. The mission statement could be written by the teacher or collaboratively by the teacher and students. The following is an example of a classroom mission statement: We will come to school on time and ready to learn. We will be responsible for our own learning. We will work hard in order to be promoted to ___ grade.

The Generic Bulletin Board

If working smarter not harder is your motto, then create a generic class bulletin board. A generic bulletin board is a great hallway or classroom display because it can stay up all year with very little maintenance. Although the generic bulletin board theme stays the same, the student work being displayed will change. Students will be in control of choosing their best work for the display.

Creating a Generic Bulletin Board

Follow these easy steps to create a generic class bulletin board that can be left up all year:

1. Establish a generic bulletin board title and theme such as:
   — Flying High in First Grade (airplane/clouds theme)
   — Second Grade's Smart Cookies (cookie theme)
   — Working Hard in Third Grade (pencil theme)
   — Fantastic Fourth Graders (star theme)
   — Fifth Grade Fundamentals (thinking bubble, or pencil theme)

2. Create and laminate a name tag for each child to match your bulletin board theme, such as a yellow star, a pencil, or light brown cookie shape. Use a permanent marker to write each child's name on a name tag.

3. Laminate and place a black piece of construction paper under each student's themed name tag. Use the black construction paper as a backing to display each student's chosen piece of work (see figure 2.1).

4. Set up a collection bin titled *My Best Work* in the classroom. Allow students to place work that is complete and free of mistakes in this bin to later be displayed. If the student already has work displayed, simply take it down, grade it, and place the new piece of work in its place.

5. At the end of the year use fingernail polish remover to erase the student names off the name tags and reuse them year after year.

Figure 2.1
The Generic Bulletin Board

Creating a Generic Bulletin Board without a Bulletin Board

If your classroom doesn't contain a bulletin board big enough to display all student work samples, or if your hallway doesn't have a bulletin board, then resort to creating a generic display without the bulletin board. The following directions and figures 2.2 and 2.3 will guide you in creating a display for all of your student's work using a large empty space on a wall:

1. Depending on how many students are in your class, purchase four to twelve hooks (the type that has an adhesive backing to stick to the wall) and clothes pins (one for each student). You will also need a roll of string (fishing line, kite string, or twine will do).

2. Underneath your chalkboard ledge strategically place your adhesive hooks to prevent your string from sagging too far as your students hang their work (refer to figures 2.2 and 2.3).

3. Write the student's names on the clothes pins.

4. Lace the string that you chose through the eye of each of the clothes pin springs. Secure the string to the adhesive hooks by tying knots.

5. Spread the student's clothes pins out evenly and far enough apart to display each student's chosen piece of work.

6. Explain to the students that they may choose to hang their best work samples on the clothes pin that bears their name. The students may change their work that is being displayed as frequently as they wish.

★**Tip:** This generic bulletin board display could be placed under a chalkboard in a classroom that lacks space or utilized by placing the display on an empty hallway wall (see figures 2.2 and 2.3). Don't forget to hang a title above the display.

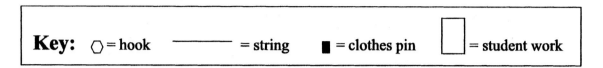

Figure 2.2
Underneath the Chalkboard Display

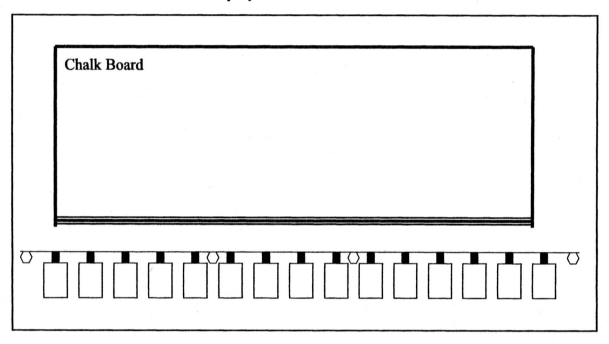

Figure 2.3
Wall Display

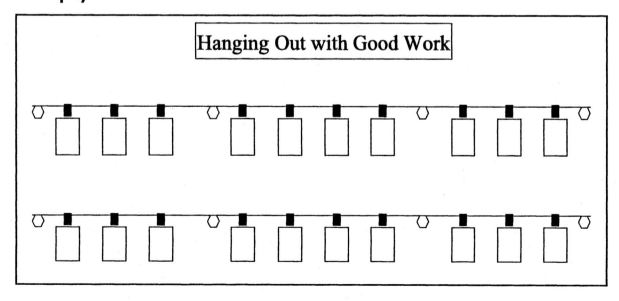

Interactive Bulletin Boards

If you enjoy maintaining bulletin boards and you don't mind updating them on a frequent or monthly basis, then the interactive bulletin board might make a great addition to your classroom. The interactive bulletin board can actually serve as a teaching tool by collaborating with students to create the display in order to introduce units, culminate units, or to complete learning activities. There are many academic possibilities for connecting student learning to the interactive bulletin board. To help establish interactive bulletin boards in your classroom use or modify the following ideas to match your curriculum needs.

Interactive Reading Bulletin Board Ideas

Interactive reading bulletin boards can help promote reading by challenging students to meet reading goals.

- Reading Is "Fun"damental:
    Each time a student reads a book they can complete a teacher-created bookmark that has space for writing the title and author of the story. The object is to promote reading by challenging students to fill the bulletin board with bookmarks.

- We Treasure Books:
    The student must read five books and then they are able to record the title of all five books on a recording sheet that is in the shape of a treasure chest. Challenge the students to see who can turn in the most treasure chests to display on the bulletin board.

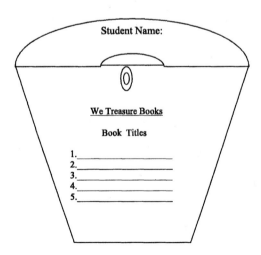

● Boasting About Books:

Students read stories and then complete a mini book report to hang on the bulletin board that provides information on the title, author, and a brief synopsis of the book that the student has read.

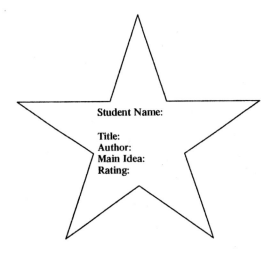

Student Name:

Title:

Author:

Brief Synopsis of the Story:

● Rating What We Read:

After completing a story, students can complete a star-shaped recording sheet for the bulletin board with space for recording the title, author, the main idea, and the rating that the student gives the book using the star scale 1-5 (five being the highest score).

Student Name:

Title:
Author:
Main Idea:
Rating:

● Get Lost... In a Good Book:

Once students have finished reading a book, they can tell about what they have read by making a book jacket (made by folding a sheet of paper in half) to hang on the bulletin board. On the cover of their book jacket they can write the title, author's name, and draw a picture of the book's main idea. Inside the book jacket students should write what the story was all about. Collect the book jackets and display them on the bulletin board.

Title:
Author:
Student Name:

Interactive Writing Bulletin Board Ideas

Completing the writing process takes a lot of time and hard work, so let the students show off their efforts by displaying their final written product. When students are aware that their work will be seen by others, they are more likely to turn in their very best work.

- Fall into Writing:

  Display fall leaves with student's names written on them and underneath each leaf hang the student's writing work. Around the display of written work, place pictures of a fall tree, acorns, and a squirrel. The display can stay up throughout the fall season, however change the student's written work frequently.

- Wonderful Winter Writers:

  Display snowflakes with student's names written on them (snowflakes could be made by the students or the teacher) and underneath each snowflake hang the student's written work. Around the display of written work place pictures of a snowman and a pine tree covered with snow. Cotton balls could be used to represent falling snow for the display.

- Spring into Writing:

  Display flowers with student's names written on them and underneath each flower hang the student's written work. Around the display of written work, place pictures of a blossoming tree (blossoms for the tree can be made with pieces of pink tissue paper), the sun, a rainbow, and a rain cloud.

- Summer Expressions:

  Display beach umbrellas with students' names written on them and underneath each beach umbrella hang the student's written work. Around the display of written work create a beach scene with pictures of sand, ocean water (blue cellophane can be used to give the water a 3-D effect), a beach ball, and a shovel and pail.

Interactive Math Bulletin Board Ideas

Math should be connected to everyday, real-life situations in order to make learning meaningful and interactive math bulletin boards can help make that connection. Here are a few examples of how:

- Math Is All Around Us:

  Introduce math at the beginning of the year by instructing students to bring in examples of *everyday math* to be placed on the bulletin board. Everyday math examples could be an empty cereal box displaying percents, a picture of a clock, a menu displaying prices, an advertisement containing a graph, etc. As the examples are brought in or after the examples are collected refer to the board to discuss the findings with the students.

- Tooth Graph:

  Display each student's name on a tooth pictograph with the question, "How many teeth have you lost this year?" Instruct students to record when they lose their teeth by placing a tooth picture above their name (tooth pictures can be printed from clip art). This graph is interactive and reinforces graphing skills throughout the year.

- Class Birthday Graph:

  Create a birthday pictograph for the whole group to record how many students' birthdays are in each month. This could be used as an icebreaker activity for students on the first day of school or completed during the graphing unit in math. The class birthday graph could stay up all year.

- The Math Master/Question of the Week:

  Design a math Question of the Week board outlined with math flashcards as a border. On a sentence strip write a question of the week related to the math unit being studied. Staple an empty expanding pocket folder underneath the question for students to place their written answer attempts. At the end of the week draw one correct answer to receive a prize.

- Speaking the Language of Math:

  Create a bulletin board that displays vocabulary words that students have been introduced to throughout each math unit. You could organize this bulletin board the same way you would a word wall with the alphabet letters A through Z and math vocabulary words displayed under each letter. Another option is to display the name of the unit that you are studying in math in the center of the bulletin board and around it place the unit's vocabulary words and their definitions as they are taught.

Interactive Social Studies Bulletin Board Ideas

Creating a social studies interactive bulletin board will provide a fun and exciting way for students to learn about themselves, other people, and places around the world.

- A Kind Word Can Make You Smile!

  Place random size smiley faces in different colors around the board. During a lesson on good citizenship have students write kind words on index cards, discuss those words and how they make you feel, and hang them on the bulletin board. Students could also keep adding kind words that aren't already displayed as they are heard or used in class.

- What Do You Know About _____ ?

  Display historical figures appropriate to the month they are celebrated and challenge students by questioning them on facts that describe those prominent figures from our past. Place an expanding pocket folder below the challenge question for students to place their answers in. Choose one correct answer at the end of each week for a prize.

● Student Spotlight:

Highlight one student's life per week using a teacher-created poster that asks questions to be answered by the student at home and brought back ready to be displayed. On the poster provide an area for the student's picture. Sample set up for the questions on the student spotlight poster could be:

My Self Portrait	**Student Spotlight**
	My name is _____.
	My hobby is _____.
	I am _____ years old.
	My favorite sport is _____.
	My favorite food is _____.
	I own a pet _____.
	My favorite book is _____.
	My favorite subject in school is _____.
	When I grow up I want to be _____.

● Places Around the World:

Throughout the Places Around the World unit students could bring in postcards from around the world to share, find on the map, and display on the board. Discussing the different postcards that are brought in each day would be a wonderful warmup activity before beginning the social studies lesson. To create this center, display the planet earth or a world map in the center of a bulletin board and request students to bring in multicultural postcards to begin a collage of postcards.

● Where Am I?

Students can practice mapping skills by placing a large map in the center of a bulletin board and having numbered questions written on sentence strips around the map that ask students to locate places using the given map coordinates. This bulletin board could be used as a center or as challenge questions for students who finish their work early.

Interactive Science Bulletin Board Ideas

Science is a very important subject which requires math and reading skills in order to be successful. Displaying an interactive science bulletin board will remind students just how important science truly is.

- The Scientific Method:

    Create the steps of the scientific process with picture icons to match (Question, Purpose, Hypothesis, Research, Experiment, Results, and Conclusion). Next, make a large picture of a light bulb to place above the step within the scientific method that students are currently working on during class science experiments. The light bulb can be held secure by a thumb tack for easy manipulation.

- Identifying _____:

    Instruct students to create and label scientific information that they have learned about during a lesson or after completing a science unit. This activity could be completed for identifying sea life, pond life, the planets, cloud formations, types of rocks, etc.

- A Diagram of the _____:

    Students could work together to create a diagram that illustrates learning that has taken place during science, such as sequencing life cycles, identifying parts of the food group pyramid, naming skeleton bones, labeling the layers of the earth, etc.

- What Do You Know About _____?

    Display the science-related topic or question in the center of the bulletin board. This bulletin board will work in the same way that a KWL what do you know, want to know, what have you learned chart would. Before studying a topic, students will tell what they know and want to know about it by writing on a sentence strip or giving a dictation. After completing the learning on the topic, students could revisit the bulletin board to answer their original questions or state new learning to add to the board.

The Word Wall

The word wall is a popular interactive bulletin board which serves as a classroom tool or spelling reference for pre-kindergarten through second grade that displays words that students have learned and must spell correctly throughout their written work. Depending on the school's focus or departmentalization, third through fifth grade may have a math, science, or social studies vocabulary wall in place of a word wall. Word walls should be large and placed in a very visible area.

Word walls may be purchased through teacher stores or education product magazines and come with the letters and words already prepared. The downfall of purchasing your word wall is that a company which is unfamiliar with your class is deciding on what words you will need for your word wall display. If you decide to purchase your word wall, look through the words that are provided and use or add words that match the vocabulary from your school district's curriculum. Most teachers choose to design their own word wall.

Designing a Word Wall

- Choose a large bulletin board, a chalkboard (if you have more than one), or mobile chalkboard on wheels to display the word wall.

- To begin the layout for a word wall or vocabulary word wall, hang the bulletin board background and create a title (Our Class Word Wall or Our Math Words).

- Letters for the word wall can be made by using a die-cut machine or you may purchase an alphabet line and cut out the letters.

- Place the letters of the alphabet in alphabetical order, in rows, and with adequate space between and below each letter for mounting words on the word wall (see figure 2.4). If you are using a magnetic chalkboard for the word wall then attach magnets to the backs of the letters and words in order to display them.

- Words for the word wall could be printed by using a large font on your word processor that resembles the print expected of your students' writing, or simply made by using a black marker and writing the words on index cards. Speak with colleagues about a mandatory word list that your class should have mastered by the end of the year and use those words to create your word wall. The Dolch high frequency word list is a widely used list throughout many school districts and contains a list of age-appropriate words for the primary grade levels. See chapter four for the Dolch word lists pre-primer through second grade.

- Add words to the word wall by placing them under the alphabet letter that matches the letter the word begins with. Only add words that students have been introduced to and had an adequate amount of time to practice (typically one week).

- An optional green background can be used for word wall words that can be decoded or sounded out. A red background can be used for words that can not be decoded.

- Another option is to cut around the word or outline the word with a red marker in order to help students focus on the *shape* of the word. Outlining the shape of the word will help students recognize what each letter should look like when writing.

Figure 2.4
Word Wall Example

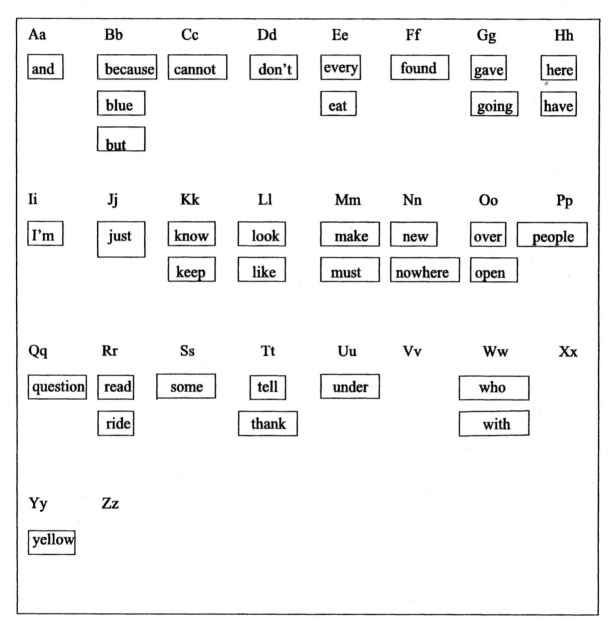

How Many Word Wall Words Should Be Displayed?

A pre-kindergarten word wall should have about 25 words and a kindergarten will have about 50 words by the end of the year. First and second grade will have about 100 to 150 word wall words by the end of the year. Refer to chapter four for the Dolch word lists. Children's names could also be included in the word wall in addition to your high frequency words. Words should be added slowly to the word wall and only added after the students have mastered the word by completing weekly word wall activities.

Word Wall Activities

Only three to five word wall words, based on your student's needs, should be introduced each week, and activities should be done with each word throughout the week before it is added to the word wall. Practicing the word wall words can be done as a whole group activity and/or as independent activities.

Whole Group Word Wall Activities

Whole group word wall activities could include introducing words during the morning news, by highlighting new words in stories or poems, exposing students to words on flash cards or in sentences, and by playing games. Word wall games can be played before reading groups, before the writing block activities, or at the end of the day. The following are whole group word wall game ideas:

- *Wordo:* Students write word wall words on a tic-tac-toe style board and place pennies on words that are called out by the teacher. The first one to get three words in a row calls out "WORDO" and wins a sticker.

- *Word Detectives:* Students number a paper 1 to 10. Next, students will listen to teacher-given clues to identify and write the word wall words that the teacher is thinking of. For example:

  — Number one, I'm thinking of a word that rhymes with man and starts with /c/. (can)

  — Number two, I'm thinking of a word that names the place where students learn. (school)

  — Number three, I'm thinking of a word that means the opposite of the word up. (down)

- *Word Wall Relay Race:* Divide the class into two teams. One student from each team will compete against each other to be the first to write the given word wall word on the chalkboard. Award points to the teams each time they are first to write the word correctly. The first team to earn ten points wins.

- *Spotlight on Words:* Turn off the classroom lights and shine a flashlight on select words on the word wall. Call on volunteers to read and use those words within oral sentences.

- *Writing Word Wall Words:* Pass out mini chalkboards with chalk or wipe boards with dry erase markers and call out words for students to find and write. Call on volunteers to spell the words as the rest of the students self-check their work.

- *Clapping Words:* The teacher calls out a word from the word wall and students then repeat the word, say the spelling of the word and simultaneously clap for each letter they say.

what: W — H — A — T

(clap) (clap) (clap) (clap)

Independent Word Wall Activities

Independent word wall activities can be incorporated into seatwork time or morning work by creating a word wall work poster like the one shown in figure 2.5. Differentiate the word wall work activities based on your students' needs. Include pictures of each expectation in order to differentiate for the struggling readers. The following are independent word wall activity ideas:

- Imagine That (students write and illustrate each word wall word of the week)
- Word Search
- Making Sense (students complete a sentence that makes sense with a word from the word box)
- Crossword Puzzles
- Word Scramble (scramble the letters from the words and challenge students to figure out the correct spelling of the word that is scrambled)
- Clue Finder (write clues for students to read in order to figure out which word the teacher is referring to)
- Short Story (students could create a short story using the selected word wall words)

Figure 2.5
Word Wall Work Poster Example

Word Wall Work

Monday:	Rainbow write the words. Write the word in pencil once. Then trace over the word five times with a different color crayon each time.
Tuesday:	Write each word 5 times each.
Wednesday:	Go on a word hunt and find each word in a book.
Thursday:	Write each word in alphabetical order.
Friday:	Write each word in a sentence.

Chapter 3
Planning Efficiently and Effectively

Everything is in place and your classroom looks great! Now it's time to plan. Planning is what makes a teacher successful so let's not waste any time before getting started. Chapter three will help you develop plans with ease for the long and short range time frames, observations, differentiation, assessments, student-teacher conferencing, organization of classroom materials, and time management.

Long Range Planning

Planning for the upcoming school year should be done first and will require a long range plan. A long range plan is a timeline for when to teach each unit and focus skill within all of the subject areas throughout the year. Depending on your preference, the long range plan can be written through the use of an outline or a table (figures 3.1 and 3.2). The long range plan examples offered in figure 3.1 and 3.2 are partial and should serve only to help you begin the set up for each month of the entire academic year. Follow these steps to generate your long range plan:

- For each subject the teacher must study the units and lesson plan suggestions within the curriculum guides, become familiar with the focus skills that students need to master for each unit's summative assessments, and know the unit timelines that have been suggested by your school district.

- Keep a school calendar readily available to reference and incorporate school closings, important dates, and hidden curriculum (holidays, celebrations of historical figures, and assemblies) into the long range plan.

- Develop a long range plan in the form of an outline or table for the entire academic year that will highlight:

    — Units of study from each subject area.

    — Focus skills that need to be taught for each subject's unit of study.

    — A time frame for teaching each unit of study and the focus skills.

- Always keep your long range plan in your plan book so that it may be referenced for planning lessons and to help you stay within each unit's time frame throughout the school year.

- Submit a copy of your long range plan to your school principal.

Figure 3.1
Sample of a Long Range Plan Format
Outline/Month to Month Example

<table>
<tr>
<td valign="top">

September/Long Range Plan

1.   Math Unit: Patterns
     14 Lessons
          Identify and Explain Patterns (5 days)
          Extend a Pattern   (5 days)
          Create a Pattern   (4 days)
          Pattern Summative Assessment (1 day)

2.   Social Studies Unit: School & Self Awareness
     20 Lessons
          School Awareness (10 days)
          All About Me (5 days)
          Families (5 days)
          School & Self Summative Assessment
          (1 day)

3.   Reading Genre: Nursery Rhymes
     Duration of September
          Mother Goose
          Poems
          Songs

4.   Johnny Appleseed Day (1 day)

</td>
<td valign="top">

October/Long Range Plan

1.   Math Unit: Graphs
     18 Lessons
          Interpret a Variety of Graphs (10 days)
          Collect and Record Data in Order to
          Create a Graph (8 days)
          Graph Summative Assessment (1 day)

2.   Science Unit: Seasonal Changes
     18 Lessons
          Fall (5 days)
          Temperature/Weather (7 days)
          Animal Adaptation (7 days)
          Seasonal Changes Summative Assessment
          (1day)

3.   Reading Genre: Fiction
     Duration of October
          Make Predictions
          Compare Texts
          Identify Realism/Fantasy
          Retell Events

4.   Christopher Columbus Day (1 day)

</td>
</tr>
</table>

Figure 3.2
Sample Long Range Plan Format
Table/Unit of Study and Focus Skills

Math Unit:	Focus Skill	# of Lessons	Start	Finish
Shapes	Identify and describe attributes of a triangle, square, circle, and rectangle.	8	8-31	9-9
	Construct shapes using geo-boards and other manipulatives.	5	9-10	9-17
	Identify and manipulate (slide, stack, and roll) 3-D shapes.	7	9-20	9-28
	Identify the line of symmetry, halves, and whole.	8	9-29	10-8
Measurement	Identify the longest and shortest given object.	4	10-11	10-14
	Measure objects with non-standard units.	3	10-15	10-19
	Measure objects using inches on a ruler.	5	10-20	10-26
	Discriminate between heavier and lighter using a balance scale.	5	10-27	11-2
Time	Identify the parts of a clock (face, minute hand, and hour hand).	2	11-3	11-4
	Identify time to the hour.	4	11-5	11-11
	Identify time to the half hour.	5	11-12	11-18
	Mixed review of time to the hour and half hour.	2	11-19	11-22

Short Range Planning

The long and short range plans go hand-in-hand. The long range plan is a general overview of the units of study and their timelines for being taught throughout the year, while the short range plan focuses on daily or weekly planning for each unit of study currently being taught. Short range plans can be in the form of a teacher lesson plan book (figure 3.3) and formal lesson plans (figure 3.4).

The Teacher's Plan Book

A teacher lesson plan book provides week-by-week planning blocks used to record daily objectives for each unit of study and important lesson information, such as materials needed. Follow these steps to generate your short range plans in the form of a teacher lesson plan book:

- Purchase a teacher lesson plan book at a local teacher materials store if your school doesn't already supply this tool for their teachers.

- Reference your district and school calendar to record the following dates in your teacher plan book:

  — school closings

  — half days

  — holidays

  — dates that each quarter will begin and end

  — scheduled field trips

  — assemblies

  — other pertinent information

- Cross reference the following when planning:

  — Your long range plan to record the unit's time frame within your plan book.

  — The unit's summative assessment and the school district's curriculum guide in order to identify focus skills that must be taught and ideas for teaching those focus skills during lessons.

  — The state curriculum to reference and write daily objectives for each lesson that will be covered throughout the upcoming week. ★**Tip:** To allow for flexibility, it is best to plan on a weekly basis, just in case there are emergency school closings or students need more or less time on a given objective.

Figure 3.3
Teacher Lesson Plan Book Example

Date	Reading	Math/Time	Writing	Science/ Life Cycles
Monday 5/5	We will retell the story by sequencing events.	We will tell time to the hour by reading given times on a clock. (lesson #3)	We will brainstorm topics for our paragraph by creating a list.	We will complete a KWL chart on butterflies in order to identify what we know and want to know about butterflies.
Tuesday 5/6	We will compare elements of realism and fantasy from the story by completing a *T-Chart*.	Telling time to the hour continued. (lesson #4)	We will discuss and write topic sentences in order to begin our rough draft.	We will analyze the life cycle of a butterfly. (butterfly video)
Wednesday 5/7	We will compare the main characters by completing a Venn diagram.	We will tell time to the half hour by writing the correct time for each given clock. (lesson #5)	We will write four detail sentences that support our topic in order to complete our rough draft.	We will sequence the life cycle of a butterfly by writing and illustrating.
Thursday 5/8	We will identify the problem and solution in the story by referring to the text.	Telling time to the half hour continued. (lesson #6)	We will proofread our paragraph by using editing marks.	We will tell what we have learned about butterflies by listing five facts.
Friday 5/9	School Closed For Teacher Planning $\longrightarrow$			

Formal Lesson Plans

A formal lesson plan is another short range plan which only needs to be written for administrators to reference during formal observations (see lesson plan example 3.4). At most schools the following process will occur when preparing for a formal lesson plan:

- The teacher will write a lesson plan.

  When writing your lesson follow your school district's required lesson plan format. If you're not sure of the format request a copy from your colleagues. A sound lesson plan will include some or all of the following components:

  1. A state curriculum indicator.

  2. A teacher-written objective that reflects the state curriculum indicator that is directly related to the outcome of the student assessment.

  3. A warm–up or engagement activity.

  4. Give a simple explanation of the lesson's objective and the enduring learning. Enduring learning occurs when a connection is made between the student's lives and the learning that is about to take place by describing how the objective is important and relates to the real world.

  5. A student exploration of or discussion on the objective which allows the teacher to assess the student's prior knowledge.

  6. Teacher and student explanation and modeling of the objective.

  7. A collaborative group practice activity that reflects the objective (whole group, small groups, or partners working together).

  8. An extended independent practice activity that reflects the objective. During this time the teacher may opt to work with a small group of students who still seem to be struggling with the objective.

  9. Student completion of a formative assessment in order to evaluate the student's learning.

  10. A review of the objective and learning that has taken place through a brief or extended response in the form of a journal entry and/or verbal responses.

  11. Assign and explain homework if applicable.

- Follow these tips when planning your formal lesson plan:
  Reference your long range plan to identify the unit that is scheduled to be taught.

  1. Look over your district's curriculum guide for the unit and the unit's summative assessment in order to identify a focus skill that must be taught.

  2. Create a formative assessment and a rubric that will verify the student's acquisition of the focus skill.

  3. Match the focus skill to a state curriculum indicator in order to identify and write the objective for the lesson that will be taught.

  4. Plan the lesson by incorporating skills that students will need in order to be successful on their formative assessment and ultimately the objective.

  5. Read the school district's purchased teacher resource guide to help generate ideas on how to teach the focus skill.

  6. If possible, allow a mentor to critique your lesson plan and assessment.

- The administrator will evaluate the lesson plan.

  1. Most principals require a pre-observation conference to discuss your objectives, the flow of your lesson, and whether or not the objective matches your assessment and lesson activities.

  2. After your pre-observation conference, the principal will observe and take notes on your lesson activities, student-teacher interaction, and the student success rate.

  3. A post-observation conference will be held between you and your principal in order to discuss your lesson and the student success rate.

- How to prepare for a post-observation conference and what to expect:

  1. Take the graded assessments from your lesson to this meeting so that you can show your lesson's student success rate.

  2. The principal will check to see if you are self-assessing your own lessons, so be ready for the principal's all time favorite post-conference questions: "How do you feel about your lesson?" "What would you do differently the next time you teach this lesson?"

  3. It is your principal's job to make sure teachers within his or her school are performing at their best, so expect to hear praise and constructive criticism. If applicable, use these critiques to make your next formal lesson plan and observation even better.

Figure 3.4
Formal Lesson Plan Example

Kindergarten Math Lesson Plan

State Curriculum Indicator Statement:
Measure using non-standard units.

State Curriculum Objective:
Students will identify and apply systems of measurements.

Kid Friendly Objective:
We will measure the weight of objects by using a balance scale and cubes.

Enduring Learning:
Students will learn why balance scales are important and how they are used in real-world experiences.

Engagement/Warm-Up Activity:
• Display a balance scale and ask students where they have seen this tool used before.
• Pose the question: Why are balance scales important?
• Predict if items on display will weigh more than an apple.
• Check predictions using a balance scale.

Explanation/Modeling:
• Teacher will explain the purpose of a balance scale.
• Teacher will use the think-aloud method to model how to weigh objects using the cubes and a balance scale.
• Repeat with other objects by having students assist.

Extension/Exploration:
• Students will be organized so they may work in small groups.
• Each group will have a balance scale, cubes, and four objects to weigh.

Evaluation/Formative Assessment:
• Students will draw one of the objects and the number of cubes they used to balance the scale during the small group activity.

Rubric:

 : The student was able to successfully draw one object which was weighed and labeled the object with the amount of cubes that was equal to and represented its weight.

 : The student was able to label the weight of the object but did not illustrate which object actually weighed that amount of cubes.

 : Did not understand the objective or did not participate.

Planning for Differentiation

Ring-a-ding-ding. What's that sound? No, it's not the dismissal bell, it's the bell curve. The bell curve represents the range of ability groups represented within your class from below average, average, to above average. It is imperative that instruction challenges and provides assistance for all students no matter what range they fall within on the bell curve. When you diversify your teaching strategies and your expectations for each child's learning to fit the student needs in your classroom, this is called differentiation. Simply put, differentiation is how you plan to challenge the successful students and help the struggling student during any given lesson. This may sound like a lot of planning but as you come to know your students' interests and abilities, differentiation becomes second nature for most teachers.

When you first begin to add differentiation to your lessons, just choose one focus such as differentiating your teaching strategies. If you teach reading groups according to student reading abilities, then you are already differentiating and you probably didn't even realize it. Below are examples of differentiation that can be easily incorporated into your lessons or daily routines. Experiment with differentiation and most of all have fun!

Challenging Students

Challenging students should not be a challenge for the teacher or seem like a *punishment* for students who finish their work early only to be loaded down with more work. Challenging students should be an opportunity to stretch the student's thinking or to keep them from sitting idle. The following ideas will help to inspire students to stretch their learning:

- Arrange for students to present concepts, peer teach, and demonstrate expectations for other students when possible during lessons.
- Provide bonus or challenge questions on the back or bottom of student assignments.
- Encourage the class to share and grow from each other's ideas by incorporating time for students to reflect on information and ask questions about the learning which has taken place.
- Require students to keep a learning log for recording written brief and extended constructed responses on concepts they have learned.
- Include books in your classroom library which could be referenced by students if they would like to seek more information on the unit or lesson topic.
- Make up an enrichment packet that students can keep in their desk and work on if they complete their assignment early.
- Time students as they complete activities or drills in order to help them practice the ability of processing and comprehending information more quickly.
- Extend the learning process by requiring students to conduct research via the Internet, access computer programs to create informative slide shows, utilize computer graphics for projects, or use the word processor to type their final product.

- Give students control over their learning by allowing them to use a rubric in order to design their own formative assessment which demonstrates their subject knowledge.

- Let students keep their own personal reading material in their desk (magazines, books of interest, or activity books such as coloring, word search, or crossword puzzle books) so they may have something more to think about if they finish assignments early.

Helping Struggling Students

Helping struggling students should not be a struggle for the teacher. The following strategies will help provide extra support for students without overwhelming the teacher:

- Provide resources to help make the student more successful such as a dictionary, hundreds chart, a calculator, a hard copy of the overhead transparency being displayed, or manipulatives.

- Give appropriate wait time as the student processes information before they are expected to answer a question. Another suggestion is to establish cues with the student who needs extra thinking time that prepares them for being called on next (tug on your ear, touch your chin, etc.).

- Build on the student's background knowledge.

- The teacher should always model expectations to ensure student understanding and success.

- Display pictures of directions or written directions on the board for students to follow.

- Give directions and pass out papers and materials in manageable steps so not to overwhelm the student.

- State the expectations clearly by providing students with a rubric.

- Have students restate the directions that were given.

- Provide exciting hands-on learning experiences.

- Give the student a highlighter to highlight important information or directions.

- Allow extra time for students to complete activities.

- Assign a partner or peer teacher to the student who needs extra support.

- Reduce the work load (this can be done by cutting the work load or a worksheet in half so the student can complete the assignment and feel successful).

- Provide extra-credit activities to help raise their grade.

- Individualize student expectations.

- Design lesson activities that build on what the student is interested in.

- Connect student learning to real-world situations so students can grasp the value and meaning of the lesson objective.

- Observe how the student learns best (visual, auditory, tactile, or kinesthetic) and teach to their strengths.

- Design lessons around small group instruction by reviewing or re-teaching concepts with students who are struggling while the rest of the class completes their formative assessment independently at their seats.

- Arrange for the student to work with a specialist such as a special educator, reading specialist, occupational therapist, speech pathologist, or even a teacher aide or volunteer in order to work on skills that they are struggling with.
- Identify goals for the student's learning by conducting teacher-student conferences.
- Reward the student for reaching his or her academic goal.

Assessments

Assessment scores drive the teacher's instruction and planning. For example, if the overall class score is high on an assessment, the teacher knows that it is time to move on to the next focus skill or unit; however if the overall class score is low on an assessment, the teacher knows that they must re-teach a lesson or spend more time on that unit before moving on to something new.

Formative Assessments

Every lesson that you plan must include a formative assessment. A formative assessment is given to students at the end of each lesson in order to evaluate their understanding of the lesson objective. The formative assessment can be a valuable diagnostic tool that provides feedback for the teacher to help determine whether or not to spend more or less time on a given focus skill.

The formative assessment can be completed independently or within cooperative groups. If students are working in groups to complete a formative assessment, then be sure to assign each student an independent job for which they will receive a grade, assuring that everyone is responsible for the work.

Formative assessment ideas:

- teacher observations/anecdotal notes
- student-teacher conferences
- oral questioning and answering
- rubrics
- complete a project
- computer tasks
- performances (role playing, skits, puppet shows)
- short written response (journal entry, labeling, reflection, paragraph)
- extended written response (report, essay, letter, synopsis)
- musical effort (write a song, poem, or rap)
- read and respond task
- cloze sentence activity (sentence starters, fill in the blank)
- matching
- multiple choice

- cut and paste
- true or false
- graphic organizers (see chapter eleven for reproducible examples)
- comprehension questions

Summative Assessments

A summative assessment should be referenced early on when planning lessons in order to identify the cumulative unit expectations that students are responsible for knowing and testing. The typical summative assessment format is that of a standardized test which is completed by the student independently and could take one or more class periods to complete. The summative assessments can provide a comparison of students within your class to each other, the class next door, and students in other schools. Since summative assessments are typically given to large quantities of students over long durations of time with no regard given to individual student background knowledge or learning styles, these tests are often considered biased. The student's academic performance should not be judged solely on their summative assessment score.

Summative assessment formats:

- selected portfolio work samples
- unit assessments
- benchmark tests
- milestone assessments
- state required standardized tests

Rubrics

Planning for how you will assess your student's performance or final product is just as important as planning the lesson. A rubric is an assessment tool which provides teachers with a non-bias method for scoring assignments and the students with a clear understanding of final product expectations.

The rubric's function is to establish detailed standards of which the student's assignment or final product must meet in order to receive the correlating score. Rubrics can be formulated in numerous ways to evaluate any final product necessary (see figures 3.5a, b, c, and d).

- When formulating a rubric remember to include the *3 S's*:

*S*cale

*S*cores

*S*tandards

● Follow these steps in order to formulate a rubric to fit your student and grading needs:

1. Consider the final product which will demonstrate the student's learning and write the objective or purpose of the lesson.

2. Establish a *scale* which will rank the student's final product achievements from excellent to incomplete and anything in between. The teacher may choose any group of three to five descriptive words to create the scale's achievement levels. Rubric *scale* examples:

   — Excellent/Good/Poor/Insufficient/No Score

   — Outstanding/Very Good/Satisfactory/Needs Improvement/No Attempt

   — Above Average/Average/Below Average/No Effort

   —Very Good/Good/Fair/No Response

3. Correlate *scores* for each achievement level within the scale of the rubric in order to provide students with an even greater understanding of how their final product will be graded. The scoring system you choose should be familiar to the students and the teacher's grade book. Possible scoring examples are:

   — checks (check plus/check/check minus)

   — smiley faces (smiley face/straight face/frown face)

   — numerals (4-3-2-1-0)

   — percentages (100% - 75% - 50% - 25% - 0%)

   — letter grades (A-B-C-D-E/F)

4. Decide on grading *standards* which will define each achievement level and score within the rubric's scale. These standards should clearly state the teacher's final product expectations. The standards can be developed by the teacher or through collaboration between teacher and students. The following are examples of word choices that could be used for defining *standards*:

   Standards Describing *Excellent* Work:

– very clear	– consistent
– no errors/correct	– effectively
– complete understanding	– answered accurately
– provides many examples	– completely
– all directions were followed	– includes
– well developed	– well organized
– always	– independently

Standards Describing *Good* Work:

- clear
- minor errors
- demonstrates understanding
- provides examples
- directions were followed
- developed
- frequently

- shows evidence of
- successfully
- communicates understanding
- demonstrates
- includes
- orders ideas
- rarely needed support

Standards Describing *Satisfactory* Work:

- reasonably clear
- some errors
- shows a basic understanding
- provides limited examples
- most of the directions were followed
- satisfactory development
- most of the time

- satisfactory response
- communicates a basic understanding
- mostly accurate
- attempts
- evidence of
- attempts to order ideas
- needed help

Standards Describing *Poor* Work:

- unclear
- major errors
- can not be understood
- unrelated
- uncertain
- poorly developed
- neglected

- almost completes task
- show no understanding
- not accurate
- some directions were followed
- fails to
- unorganized ideas
- incomplete/partial

Standards Describing *Incomplete* or *Unacceptable* Work:

- shows no understanding
- didn't participate
- directions were not followed

- didn't attempt task
- illegible
- incomplete/partial

5. Provide or discuss examples of excellent, poor, and incomplete final products for students to review. Reviewing these examples will prepare students for what will be expected from the assignment and helps students understand how the rubric is utilized to grade the final product.

Figure 3.5a
Reading Rubric Example

Comprehension Rubric

We will retell the story by describing the beginning, middle, and end events.

4
Excellent:
- Accurately recalled the beginning, middle, and end events.
- Independently recalled events/not prompted.

3
Good:
- Successfully recalled the beginning, middle, and end events.
- Recalled events/rarely needed to be prompted.

2
Satisfactory:
- Communicated a basic understanding of the beginning, middle, and end events.
- Recalled events/needed to be prompted or had to reference the text.

1
Poor:
- Demonstrated a partial understanding of the story events.
- Partial recollection of the story/prompting did not help.

0
Unacceptable:
- Did not participate.

Figure 3.5b
Writing Rubric Example

Writing

We will construct a paragraph in order to demonstrate our writing skills.

4=Outstanding   3=Above Average   2=Average   1=Below Average   0=No Attempt

Grammar
4 - Always uses proper grammar.
3 - Mostly uses proper grammar.
2 - Sometimes uses proper grammar.
1 - Rarely uses proper grammar.
0 - No attempt/illegible.

Topic Sentence
4 - Very clear topic sentence that captures the audience's attention.
3 - Clear topic sentence.
2 - Understandable topic sentence.
1 - Unclear topic sentence.
0 - No attempt/illegible.

Supporting Details
4 - Includes 4 supporting details.
3 - Includes 3 supporting details.
2 - Includes 2 supporting details.
1 - Includes 1 supporting detail.
0 - Includes no details/illegible.

Conclusion
4 - Well developed concluding sentence.
3 - Developed concluding sentence.
2 - Satisfactory concluding sentence.
1 - Poorly developed concluding sentence.
0 - No attempt/illegible.

Figure 3.5c
Math Rubric Example

Math Rubric for Long Division
We will demonstrate an understanding of long division by showing our strategy.

3 = Good
- Problems are solved completely and correctly/no errors.
- The strategy is evident/all work is shown.

2 = Satisfactory
- Problems are solved completely with minor errors.
- The strategy is understood/most work is shown.

1 = Poor
- Problems are not solved completely/major errors.
- The strategy is unclear/little or no work is shown.

0 = Not Demonstrating
- Did not attempt.
- Shows no understanding.

Figure 3.5d
Science Rubric Example

Science Experiment
We will use scientific equipment in order to research a hypothesis.

A = Superior Scientist
- Performed experiment independently.
- Well developed observations are recorded.
- The conclusion provides a well developed understanding of experiment results.

B = Great Scientist
- Performed experiment with little assistance.
- Developed observations are recorded.
- The conclusion provides an understanding of the experiment results.

C = Becoming a Scientist
- Performed experiment with assistance.
- Satisfactory observations are recorded.
- The conclusion provides a reasonable understanding of the experiment results.

D = Needs to Work Harder
- Did not complete or follow the experiment directions.
- Incorrect observations and conclusion recorded.

Student-Teacher Conferencing

Planning a time for student-teacher conferences will play an integral part in a student's learning experience. Conferencing allows the teacher and student to work one-on-one to help develop the student into a lifelong independent learner. Advantages and tips for conducting student-teacher conferences:

- Student-teacher conferences develop the student's ability to self-evaluate and reflect on their academic strengths and areas of needed improvement in order for them to set personal learning goals either independently or cooperatively with the teacher.

- Students are held accountable for their learning when they are required to meet one-on-one with their teacher to discuss the learning which has transpired.

- Conferences inform students on what the teacher will ultimately expect from their final product efforts or behaviors.

- Teacher feedback which is given during conferences will help students become more successful and increase their grade point average.

- Conferencing will provide time for the teacher to obtain valuable information on student learning so they are better able to diagnostically select focus skills which need to be taught or reviewed.

- Conference time could be used for building portfolios and conducting one-on-one student-teacher discussions on:

  — writing skills (the writing process, attention to audience, grammar, neatness).

  — reading skills (reading strategies, fluency, voice inflection, comprehension, and running records).

  — math skills (student understanding of mathematical concepts and processes).

  — behavior modifications (behavior charts, stress/anger management).

- Scheduling ideas for student-teacher conferences are as follows:

  — Writing conferences can convene during the writing block while the rest of the class works to write or revise their writing assignment.

  — Reading conferences should occur during DEAR (Drop Everything and Read) or SSR time (Sustained Silent Reading) while the rest of the class independently reads a book or magazine of their choice.

  — Math conferences can be conducted while students are working on their formative assessment or while students reflect in their math journals.

  — Behavior modification conferences can be held in the morning before announcements or while students complete their assigned morning activity.

- Tips for conducting successful teacher-student conferences:
  1. Explain the purpose of student-teacher conferences so students understand why this designated time is important for their educational success.

  2. Differentiate the student-teacher conference topic of discussion according to each individual student's academic needs or behavioral concerns.

  3. Begin conferencing with students as soon as possible. Meeting with students shortly after the academic school year has begun will prove to be beneficial for planning units and lessons since it helps teachers identify what the strengths and weaknesses are of their student majority.

  4. Design and maintain a student-teacher conference schedule which allows you to meet regularly with each student. An ideal situation would be to meet with each student twice a month. The teacher should meet with the student once for a pre-conference to set learning goals and once again for a post-conference to discuss the student's accomplishments and future learning goals.

  5. Provide a focus for your student-teacher conferences by generating a *Student Goals Questionnaire* (see figures 3.6a and b) which lists topics of discussion as students set learning goals, reflect on their learning accomplishments, and decide on new goals.

  6. Reiterate the purpose of student-teacher conferences with the students so they understand that they are working toward becoming lifelong learners by developing their ability to independently analyze their learning abilities through the use of reflective questioning. Reflective questioning and focus ideas for pre- and post-conference discussions are:

     – What will my learning goal be and how do I plan to meet that goal?

     – Did I meet my learning goal?

     – How do I feel about my final product or behavior progress?

     – Did I do my very best? Why or why not?

     – What will be my future goal?

  7. Acknowledge the student's hard work by providing feedback, positive praise, and rewarding them for achieving their goals. A small reward which will go a long way could be as simple as giving the student a sticker and a few words of encouragement.

  8. Once the *Goals Conference Questionnaire* has been completed and dated, attach it to the final product and archive it within the student's portfolio in order to document and reference academic or behavioral progress with students, parents, and administrators quickly and efficiently.

Figure 3.6a
Primary Student-Teacher Goals Conference Questionnaire

<u>Student Goals Questionnaire</u>

Name:

Date:

Assignment:

My Goal:

This is my best work.   ☐ Yes   ☐ No

This   is   **/**   is not   my best work because …

My new goal:

Figure 3.6b
Intermediate Student-Teacher Goals Conference Questionnaire

Student Goals Questionnaire

Name:

Date of pre-conference:

Assignment or task:

My Goals:

Date of post-conference:

I met my goals.   ☐ Yes   ☐ No

I am really good at:

I am working on:

Teacher Comments:

The Organized Teacher

Even the most well planned lesson can go terribly wrong if what you need to implement the lesson can't be found quickly. Something as simple as walking away from the group to look for a book or manipulatives could stir your students into a commotion and distract them from learning. To prevent this scenario from occurring during instruction, you must always be prepared, and the best way to be prepared is to be organized. Use the following tips for organization:

Subject Bins

Preparing subject bins will prove to be a valuable method of organization that will keep you prepared for each lesson that you will teach throughout the day. The purpose of subject bins is to contain everything the teacher needs to teach at their fingertips, such as each subject's curriculum, lesson plans, and necessary teaching tools. Just pick up your subject bin and teach. How to set up subject bins:

1. Purchase plastic bins with a depth of at least 5 inches and the length and width of at least 14 inches (plastic dishpans work best).

2. Label each bin according to the subject content it will contain.

3. In each subject bin store lesson plans, curriculum guides, activity sheets, work books, and manipulatives that you will need throughout the day as you teach each subject.

4. Place the subject bins on a countertop for easy access.

5. When you're ready to teach each subject, just grab the subject bin and go.

Theme Containers

The early childhood educator should purchase ten one-gallon plastic containers (one for each month) for storage purposes. Label each container with the name of a month and the contents according to the theme and holiday materials it holds. Contents may consist of holiday decorations and items, books related to the themes or holidays, and center activities for the month.

Organizing Math Manipulatives

Identify the math units that you will teach by reading the math curriculum guides or your long range math plans. Purchase plastic bins with lids for storing manipulatives needed for teaching each math unit. Label each container with the math content it will hold. ★**Tip:** Before purchasing the plastic bins, take inventory of your manipulatives and decide on the number of bins needed and the necessary sizes. Store the bins above or inside of cabinets or closets.

Labeling Doors and Drawers

There are numerous supplies that teachers and students use. Most classrooms contain a lot of storage space such as drawers, closets, and cabinets. All of this storage area is great until you need something and can't find it because you don't remember which drawer or door it is hiding behind. To solve this dilemma, label the fronts of every drawer and door on your desk and closets with the content that lies behind it. Label the drawers and doors using a label machine or masking tape and a black marker. Always use storage labels and never write directly on your doors and drawers with a marker. Sample storage labels: stickers, stamps, tape, glue, writing paper, construction paper, markers, posters, sentence strips, tissues, soap, paper plates, cups, napkins, pencils, erasers, scissors, chalk, sticky notes, paper clips, magnets, calendar materials, baggies.

Time Management

Time management is a learned behavior that can help balance the time you spend at school and home. Most teachers leave the profession because they spend more time at school working than they do at home with their family. Spending too much time at school is typically mislabeled by teachers as dedication, when in fact it is mismanagement of time. Maximize the use of your professional time by establishing a daily routine, writing a *To-Do* list, and grading papers efficiently.

Establish a Routine:

- Establish a routine or time frame for completing tasks that must be done on a daily basis... no matter what. To do this make a list of time frames that you are able to complete tasks within, and within those time frames list daily tasks that you can realistically complete (see figure 3.7).
- If you stay consistent, soon your routine should become innate and you won't need to refer to your list anymore.
- Try out different routines until you find one that is efficient and works for you.

Figure 3.7
Example of Teacher Routine

DAILY TEACHER ROUTINE

Before the Morning Bell:
- Sign in
- Check E-Mails
- Check Teacher Mailbox

Before Announcements:
- Check Homework
- Record Who Completed the Homework

After Announcements:
- Attendance
- Lunch Count

During Center Clean-Up Time:
- File Originals
- Respond to Office Paperwork

During Independent Reading:
- Check Center Work and/or Seatwork

During Lunch Time:
- Return/Make Phone Calls to Parents
- Respond to Parent Notes/E-mails

During Planning Time:
- Plan for Tomorrow's Lessons
- Check Papers/Record the Scores
- Check E-mails Again

During Student Pack-Up Time:
- Update Tomorrow's Schedule/Objectives
- Complete Behavior Charts
- Return Graded Papers

After Dismissal Bell:
(30 minutes maximum)
- Prepare Tomorrow's Centers
- Prepare Subject Bins with Tomorrow's Lesson Materials

Write a To-Do List:

- Make a *To-Do* list by writing down what you wish to accomplish outside of your daily teacher routine (see figure 3.8). Cross off each task as you complete it. Any task on this list that doesn't get done can be put off until tomorrow or the day after that.

- Do not add anything to your *To-Do* list that you can't handle. If a colleague asks you to take on a responsibility that is not feasible then politely say, "Sorry, my plate is full right now but maybe I can help out next time."

Figure 3.8
Teacher *To-Do* List

TO-DO LIST

- Complete Report Cards

- Prepare Writing Presentation for the Faculty Meeting

- Collect the Reading Group Anthologies from the Book Closet

- Get One Pack of Writing Paper

- Plan the Field Trip to the Zoo

Grading Papers Efficiently:

Grading papers should not be a laborious process, so grade assignments quickly and efficiently by following these grading tricks of the trade:

- Group and grade the same assignments together so that your thought process is quick when identifying correct and incorrect answers.

- Walk around and grade the formative assessments as the students complete them. Grading papers immediately ensures better work quality, gives the student immediate feedback, and gives you less paperwork to grade later. If you are wondering how you will record grades if you haven't collected the work, do either of two things: remember the students who struggled or didn't complete the activities correctly when recording the success rate in your grade book; only collect the papers that were incorrect and record the grades accordingly.

- When grading larger assignments such as reports or essays, ration your grading workload by grading five papers per night for a week until the job is done. This is also a great strategy for completing report cards.

- Let a homework helper grade homework in the morning. Let another homework helper record who turned in homework and who did not. Only allow students to be the homework helper if they have completed their homework.

- Allow the students to help out with the grading. Have students switch papers with another classmate after they complete their assignment. Then work with the students to identify and mark the correct answers and incorrect answers. Collect the papers and record the grades.

- Not every paper turned in by your students will need to be graded with in-depth details such as editing marks and written comments. If the paper is not going to be reflected in your grade book then refrain from investing as much time grading the paper as if it were.

- Acceptable activities completed by students during center time may just receive a sticker which states an acknowledgement that the student completed their assignment.

Realizations:

In order to plan effectively and to avoid *burning out* at an early stage in your teaching career, you must come to several realizations:

- You do not need to have a bag on your shoulder or to tow a cart behind you to be a good teacher. Leave your school work at school, unless it is absolutely imperative to complete something for a deadline.

- You are not in competition with the teacher next door. If your colleague has a *cute* room and makes cute things for her students and spends every waking moment trying to out *cute* herself, well, that's her lesson to learn. Being exposed to *cute* lessons that the teacher has spent endless hours creating won't help one group of students learn any better than the rest, but being exposed to interactive lessons that require the student to do all of the work will show successful results.

- If you are working harder than your students, then you are defeating the purpose of your job. So don't cut out thirty construction paper butterflies in assorted colors and expect the students to only glue on a couple of wiggly eyes; instead give them written directions and a butterfly stencil so they can do all the work… the students are the ones in school—not you!

- If a colleague criticizes you for getting out of work on time, don't feel guilty and don't take it to heart. Your co-worker just hasn't mastered time management yet.

- Working with children all day makes some adults feel isolated, causing some teachers to crave an adult conversation by the end of the school day. Conversing with colleagues is fine, but it should be limited because the longer you talk the less time you have for planning—unless you plan to stay at school throughout the evening.

- A student has to want to learn, which makes it hard to reach every student. Of course you will do your best to reach and teach each and every student no matter what challenges they may throw your way, but you can only mold the clay that you are given. In teaching, a small success is a great success!

- No, you can't take your precious darlings home with you. Yes, you will feel sorry for some students and the lives that they go home to each night, but unless the child is being abused, it is out of your hands. Just take comfort in the fact that they are with you for most of the day in an environment that provides care, nourishment, and safety.

Chapter 4
Record Keeping Made Simple

After you have delivered your instruction, you must assess and record what the students have learned. Record keeping or documenting student progress is a part of teacher accountability. Documenting student progress can take on many forms, such as student portfolios, anecdotal notes, grade books, check sheets, and data binders. Chapter four makes record keeping simple by giving a detailed description of each type of documentation along with examples that can be used in the classroom.

Student Portfolios

Portfolios are personal folders kept for each student that contain work samples and forms that have been used to critique the student's learning in order to document the student's progress over time. The student portfolio's design and implementation possibilities are limitless. Student portfolio ideas:

- Work samples for the portfolio can be determined by the teacher, student, or both.
- Photocopy or include photographs of artifacts that students don't want to part with or are too large to file within the student portfolio.
- Date every artifact that is archived within the portfolio for progress documentation purposes.
- Review the portfolio work samples with each student by conducting student-teacher conferences. Discuss and evaluate the work samples by completing a *Goals Conference Questionnaire.* For information on how to conduct student-teacher conferences and examples of *Goal Conference Questionnaires,* refer to chapter three.
- Other than work samples, a portfolio may also include completed behavior management charts, IEP information, important paperwork, parent-teacher communication, completed conference outlines, checklists, and anecdotal notes.
- The work contained in the portfolio can be used during parent-teacher conferences and IEP meetings to illustrate the student's academic progress over time.
- A few portfolio design ideas for collecting student work samples are as follows:
  - Organize hanging file folders and tabbed manila folders labeled with each student's name within a file cabinet or portable file holder.
  - Manage portfolios through the use of pizza boxes, cereal boxes, large shoe boxes, or plastic bins with lids which have been decorated uniquely by the student and labeled with their full name.

Anecdotal Notes

Anecdotal notes are short summaries that describe the teacher's observation of student learning or behavior issues. The purpose of anecdotal notes is to go beyond just assigning the grade for an activity and instead gives a detailed and dated account of a student's interactions, behaviors, learning, and thought process that the teacher has observed. Anecdotal notes could be stored in the student's portfolio or copied and attached to the activity and sent home for parent review. Ideas for writing anecdotal notes:

- For each anecdotal note you must always write the date and, if necessary, the time when the learning activity was completed or the behavior incident occurred.

- Anecdotal notes can be written directly on student class work or on sticky notes. Start a collection of anecdotal sticky notes by attaching them to a blank sheet of paper that is labeled for the subject that the notes were taken for and then place this sheet of paper in the student's portfolio. Add anecdotal sticky notes which document the date, focus skill, and teacher observations to the student's data collection as they are made. The following are sticky note samples of anecdotal documentation written during a sorting activity:

Jake 4-19

Sorting —

Said, "I can sort by color" but he mixed the colors while sorting.

Isabel 4-19

Sorting —

Could only sort by color not shape.

Tyrell 4-19

Sorting —

Began making a pattern, had to be prompted/reminded of the definition for sorting and then she was able to sort by color and shape.

José 4-19

Sorting —

Seemed unsure, kept looking for encouragement, sorted by shapes.

- Anecdotal notes will need to be written on a daily basis for students who continually act inappropriately or demonstrate unacceptable behaviors. Anecdotal notes on behavior should be recorded in a spiral notebook or printed from your word processor and saved to a disk. When recording observations on behavior issues, only write the facts of what has been observed and never include your emotions or speculations as to why the behavior is occurring in your classroom. This may seem like a lot of work, but it is necessary to properly defend your case against student behavior interruptions when dealing with parents and administrators. You are more likely to receive assistance and support if you have proof of an ongoing problem. The following is a spiral notebook example of anecdotal documentation on a student who is demonstrating daily behavior issues:

Observations on Johnny Applecake

9-7-2010
Johnny refused to stay on his mat during quiet time. He was asked to stay on his mat several times. He continued to walk and hide around the classroom. Johnny was asked to make a choice, stay on his mat and read a book or move his behavior card. Johnny did not respond and refused to make a choice. I told him that either he could move his behavior card or I would. Johnny stood in front of the behavior chart with his hands folded in order to block me from moving his card. His card was moved and he still wandered around the classroom and continued to hide in cubbies. The guidance counselor was contacted and she intervened by taking him to her office to discuss his behavior. I sent a note home to the parents regarding the issue. Parents did not respond to the note and a message was left on their home answering machine regarding the matter.

9-8-2010
Johnny refused to stay on his mat during quiet time. He wandered around the room, sat in his cubby, and began playing in housekeeping center. He was asked several times to make a good choice and he refused. As I moved his behavior card he began taking items off of my desk and threw them onto the ground. When it was time to pack up to go home Johnny refused and threw himself down on the ground. He got in line after the other students had lined up. I contacted Johnny's mom on her cell phone. I told of the incidents that took place today and yesterday and she assured me that she would talk to Johnny and she hoped it wouldn't happen again.

9-9-2010
Johnny refused to do any math work. I saved his work to be completed during recess. After completing our math lesson I asked students to have a seat for calendar time. Johnny brought his scissors to the carpet area. I told him to put the scissors back and he threw them across the room and stomped his foot at me. I called the principal to have Johnny removed from the classroom due to unsafe behavior. The principal called home and spoke with Johnny's father about the incident.

9-10-2010
I picked up the students from their library special. Johnny refused to join the line with the other students. Johnny was asked to make a good choice and line up so that he wouldn't lose any recess time. Johnny chose to line up but he went to the front of the line and stood next to our line leader. I asked Johnny to get in line behind the line leader so that we could leave. He then ran out of the library and down the hall to our classroom. I sent a messenger to the office and the principal removed Johnny from our classroom and called the parents to schedule a meeting.

- When teacher observation is necessary for a class assessment, the most efficient method is to generate a class recording sheet (see figure 4.1). If you would like to later include each child's anecdotal note in the student portfolios then cut the class recording sheet and glue each student's strip of paper that contains written information about their performance onto the labeled sheet of paper for which subject you are collecting anecdotal notes on. More cut and paste anecdotal strips of paper or sticky notes with written anecdotes can be added to the blank sheet of paper as necessary.

Figure 4.1
Anecdotal Notes Class Recording Sheet

Anecdotal Notes		
Subject_____ Assessment _____		
Student Name	**Date**	**Observations**

Keeping a Grade Book

Teachers are accountable for tracking each student's academic progress and for documenting this data in a grade book. Documenting scores earned through class work, assessments, projects, homework, and participation will justify grades that each student will receive on his or her report card. Setting up a grade book:

1. Open your grade book to the first subject page or copy the grade book pages in figure 4.2 and place them in the grade book section of your data binder. Within the appropriate boxes, write the name of the subject and the student names in alphabetical order for which you will be recording grades. Continue this process for each subject that you will teach. Skip enough pages in between each subject in your grade book or add enough pages to your data binder in order to have room for continuing the grading process for each quarter.

2. Under each subject title write the scoring key that your grading system will follow.

3. Match your grade book to your school's report card. Since the grades that are given on the report cards are the grades that need to be justified by your grade book, it is most important that the two match. To prepare your grade book:

   — Choose the skills within each subject that must be mastered on the report card as the grading umbrellas.

   — Under each report card skill umbrella, write at least five assessments that will grade students on their achievement of this report card skill. To help jog your memory for each assignment, give a brief description such as: *Addition to 10/WB p.102* or *Adding Nickels & Dime/Mock School Store Activity.*

   — Record student grades frequently so that you don't get overwhelmed with grading too much at once.

Figure 4.2
Example of Grade Book Set Up

Subject: Quarter ____ Grading Key: Students:	Report Card Skill Assessment:	Report Card Skill:					Report Card Skill:					Report Card Skill:				
1																
2																
3																
4																
5																
6																
7																
8																
9																
10																
11																
12																
13																
14																
15.																
16.																
17.																
18.																
19.																
20.																
21.																
22.																
23.																
24.																
25.																

Report Card Skill:	Report Card Skill:	Report Card Skill:	Report Card Skill:	

Check Sheets

Organizing a check sheet is a quick and easy method for gathering student data observed for one or more skills at a time. The check sheet should have a column for student names, the date observations are made, and the learning behaviors to be observed. The teacher simply clips the check sheet to a clip board and walks about the room checking the behavior columns that are observed for each student. Data from the check sheet can then be stored appropriately in the data binder or translated into a grade for the grade book.

Figure 4.3
Student Check Sheet

Subject:	Student Check Sheet ✔ = Student has acquired the skill.			
Student Names	**Date**	**Skill #1** Description:	**Skill #2** Description:	**Skill #3** Description:

Data Binders

Data binders are three-ring binders that house information on student learning. Some teachers use data binders and a grade book to track student progress. Other teachers choose only to use a data binder by including spread sheets on their word processor for recording student grades and progress. The decision to use a data binder, grade book, or both is based on the teacher's needs. Organizing your data binder is as simple as adding a table of contents, tabbed dividers, and labels for the tabbed sections. Ideas for data binder contents:

- A grade book section and grading key (figure 4.2)
- A sample report card for teacher reference
- Spread sheets for documentation of student progress (figure 4.4)
- Student information sheets that include the child's birthday, parent names, address, phone number, allergies, and their bus number (see p. 106)
- A parent-teacher contact log (figure 4.6)
- Unit assessment scores (figures 4.5, 4.7–4.10)
- IEP information (figure 4.11)
- Anecdotal notes on student progress or behavior issues (see pgs 64–66)
- Running Record scores (figure 4.12)
- Lists of student groupings that have been made for guided reading
- Gifted and Talented information
- Report cards/comment sheets
- Parent-teacher conference outlines (see p. 160)
- Class check sheets (figure 4.3)
- Student questionnaire/goals (see pgs 55–56)
- Long range plans (see pgs 36–38)

Figure 4.4
Data Binder/Progress Documentation

Subject: Unit ____ Grading Key: Students	Focus Skill Assessment:	Unit Focus Skill:					Unit Focus Skill:					Unit Focus Skill:				
1.																
2.																
3.																
4.																
5.																
6.																
7.																
8.																
9.																
10.																
11.																
12.																
13.																
14.																
15.																
16.																
17.																
18.																
19.																
20.																
21.																
22.																
23.																
24.																
25.																
26.																

Focus Skill:					Focus Skill:					Focus Skill:					Focus Skill:					Summative Assessment	Average

Figure 4.5a
Alphabet/Sound Recognition

Student Name: Grade:				
Capital Letters	Recognition	Associates Sound to Letter	Lowercase Letters	Recognition
F			f	
C			c	
D			d	
B			b	
A			a	
E			e	
H			h	
I			i	
G			g	
K			k	
J			j	
N			n	
L			l	
M			m	
P			p	
O			o	
S			s	
R			r	
U			u	
T			t	
Q			q	
V			v	
Z			z	
W			w	
Y			y	
X			x	

Figure 4.5b
Letter Identification Chart Used for Testing Students

F	C	D	B	A
E	H	I	G	K
J	N	L	M	P
O	S	R	U	T
Q	V	Z	W	Y
X				

f	c	d	b	a
e	h	i	g	k
j	n	l	m	p
o	s	r	u	t
q	v	z	w	y
x				

Figure 4.6
Parent-Teacher Contact Log

Parent-Teacher Contact Log For the Month of _____.			
Parent Contact Data For:	Phone Call or E-Mail	Note Home	Conference
	Dates of Contact	Dates of Contact	Dates of Contact
1.			
2.			
3.			
4.			
5.			
6.			
7			
8.			
9			
10			
11.			
12.			
13.			
14			
15.			
16.			
17.			
18.			
19.			
20.			
21.			
22.			
23.			
24.			
25.			
26.			
27.			
28.			
29.			
30.			

Figure 4.7
Pre-K Assessment

Language Acquisition	Dates of Assessment				Math Skills	Dates of Assessment			
Verbally Expresses Thoughts and Feelings					Identifies Colors				
Identifies Capital Letters					Identifies Numerals 0-10				
Identifies Lowercase Letters					Counts by Rote to _____.				
Listens Attentively to a Story					Identifies Shapes				
States and Identifies First and Last Name					Can Count Sets Up to 10				

Gross Motor Skills	Dates of Assessment				Fine Motor Skills	Dates of Assessment			
Walks Correctly					Can Stack / Balance Blocks on One Another				
Runs Correctly					Uses Pencils and Crayons Independently				
Hops and Jumps Correctly					Can Cut Paper with Scissors				
Can Catch and Toss Correctly					Scribbles or Attempts to Draw or Write				
Can Use the Bathroom Independently					Can Hold a Book and Turn Pages Independently				

Figure 4.8a
Kindergarten Assessment

Reading/Writing Acquisition	Dates of Assessment			Math Skills	Dates of Assessment		
Identifies Capital Letters				Identifies Numerals 0-10			
Identifies Lowercase Letters				Identifies Numerals 11-20			
Holds a Book and Turns Pages Correctly				Identifies Color Words			
Tracks Print				Identifies Number Words			
Identifies Beginning and Ending Sounds in Words				Counts by Rote to _____.			
Can Identify Parts of a Word				Identifies Shapes by Name			
Knows the Difference Between Letters and Words				Can Sort Objects			
Identifies and Uses Reading Strategies				Identifies and Extends Patterns			
Recalls Story Events				Can Add Numbers With Sums to 10			
Recognizes High Frequency Words				Writes Numerals to 20			

Figure 4.8b
Kindergarten Assessment

Language Acquisition	Dates of Assessment				Motor Skills	Dates of Assessment			
States Full Name					Uses/Grips Pencil Correctly				
Knows Their Birthday					Uses/Grips Scissors Correctly				
Knows Phone Number					Can Trace				
Knows Address					Can Copy from Far and Near Point				
Participates in Group Discussions					Colors Appropriately				
Talks in Complete Sentences					Draws Shapes Correctly				
Speaks Using Appropriate Articulation					Can Snap, Button, and Zip				
Responds Appropriately When Spoken to					Can Hop, Jump, and Skip				
Asks Questions					Demonstrates Balance				
Can Repeat Directions					Can Catch and Toss				
Can Follow 3-Step Directions					Can Run Correctly				
Listens Attentively					Can Walk Correctly				

Figure 4.9
First Grade Assessment

Reading	Dates of Assessment				Writing	Dates of Assessment			
Identifies Capital Letters					Can Write Uppercase Letters				
Identifies Lowercase Letters					Can Write Lowercase Letters				
Associates Sounds with Letters					Can Copy from Far and Near Point				
Recognizes High Frequency Words					Reproduces Words in Left to Right Sequence				
Identifies Rhyming Words					Writes Words Phonetically				
Identifies Beginning, Middle, and End Sounds in Words					Spells Sight Words Correctly				
Identifies Word Families (at, an, am, ig)					Writes More Than One Sentence				
Identifies Diagraphs (th, ch, sh)					Uses Simple Punctuation Marks				
Segments Words by Clapping Syllables					Writes Legibly with Appropriate Spacing				
Uses Reading Strategies					Applies Capital Letters Appropriately in Words and Sentences				
Demonstrates Comprehension					Can Run Correctly				

Figure 4.10a
Dolch Word List (Pre-Primer)

Word:	Date of Mastery:
a	
and	
away	
big	
blue	
can	
come	
down	
find	
for	
funny	
go	
help	
here	
I	
in	
is	
it	
jump	
little	
look	
make	
me	
my	
not	
one	
play	
red	
run	
said	
see	
the	
three	
to	
two	
up	
we	
where	
yellow	
you	

Figure 4.10b
Dolch Word List (Primer)

Word:	Date of Mastery:	Word:	Date of Mastery:
all		was	
am		well	
are		went	
at		what	
ate		white	
be		who	
black		will	
brown		with	
but		yes	
came			
did			
go			
eat			
four			
get			
good			
have			
he			
into			
like			
must			
new			
no			
now			
on			
our			
out			
please			
pretty			
ran			
ride			
saw			
say			
she			
so			
soon			
that			
there			
this			
too			
under			
want			

Figure 4.10c
Dolch Word List (First Grade)

Word:	Date of Mastery:
after	
again	
an	
any	
as	
ask	
by	
could	
every	
fly	
from	
give	
going	
had	
has	
her	
him	
his	
how	
just	
know	
let	
live	
may	
of	
old	
once	
open	
over	
put	
round	
some	
stop	
take	
thank	
them	
then	
think	
walk	
were	
when	

Figure 4.10d
Dolch Word List (Second Grade)

Word:	Date of Mastery:	Word:	Date of Mastery:
always		wish	
around		work	
because		would	
been		write	
before		your	
best			
both			
buy			
call			
cold			
does			
don't			
fast			
first			
five			
found			
gave			
goes			
green			
its			
made			
many			
off			
or			
pull			
read			
right			
sing			
sit			
sleep			
tell			
their			
these			
those			
upon			
us			
use			
very			
wash			
which			
why			

Figure 4.11
Teacher Report/IEP or TEAM Referral

Teacher Report
_____ Teacher Signature Student Name: Birthday: Guardian Names:
Reading Comments Strengths: Needed Improvement:
Writing Comments Strengths: Needed Improvement:
Math Comments Strengths: Needed Improvement:
Behavioral Comments
Teacher Intervention Strategies Strategies: Strategies began on ___ / ___ / ___.   Results of intervention:
Suggestions Given During the Meeting   Follow-up date to discuss student progress ___ / ___ / ___.

Figure 4.12
Running Record Scores

	Running Record Scores				
Text Difficulty: **Easy = 95 - 100%** **Instructional = 90 - 94%** **Hard / Frustration Level = 80 - 89%**					
Student Names:	**Beginning of Quarter 1**	**End of Quarter 1**	**End of Quarter 2**	**End of Quarter 3**	**End of Quarter 4**

Chapter 5
Substitute Plans in a Snap

The show must go on! You never know when you're going to get sick, hurt, or have car trouble, so it is imperative to prepare emergency substitute plans. A week's worth of substitute plans should always be available and easy for the substitute to locate. Chapter five will help you prepare substitute plans in a snap by providing step-by-step instructions and ready-to-use lesson plans that require no preparation on your part.

Preparing Emergency Substitute Plans

- Purchase a three-ring binder with a clear front cover insert pocket.
- Design a cover that states:

  _____'s Substitute Plans

  Grade _____

  Room # _____

- Display the cover page by sliding it into the binder's front cover insert pocket.
- Create a table of contents and tabbed/labeled sections for organization to include:
  Section 1......Student Roster
  Section 2......Emergency Information
  Section 3......Classroom Rules and Routines
  Section 4......Substitute Plans Set A
  Section 5......Substitute Plans Set B
  Section 6......Substitute Plans Set C
  Section 7......Substitute Plans Set D
  Section 8......Substitute Plans Set E

★**Tip:** To let the substitute know which set of substitute plans to use for the day, place a sticky note so that it is visible on the tabbed section that represents the correct set of substitute plans to use that reads: "Please use these plans today."

- Section Two… *Emergency Information* should include the following:
  — fire drill route and procedure
  — bus/walker information
  — bomb threats
  — reacting to suspicious persons in the building
  — severe weather procedures
  — emergency closing/delay information
  — a map of the school indicating the location of the special area classes (music, gym, library, computer lab, art).

- Section Three... *Classroom Rules and Routines* should include the following information:

  –classroom rules

  –discipline procedures

  –bathroom and drink routines

- Sections Four through Eight... *Substitute Lesson Plans* should follow the cover page and format suggestions shown in figures 5.1 and 5.2.

- The sub plans should be generic and not require any preparation on your part or the substitute's. The substitute will need access to both plain and lined paper for students to complete activities. This paper supply should be plentiful at all times, and the location of this paper must be mentioned within the cover page of your substitute plans (reference first paragraph in figure 5.1).

- Use the generic sub plans shown in the 5.3 figures by altering the content to fit the needs of your students and by sequencing the activities to match your schedule using the format shown in figure 5.2.

- There will be no need to update your emergency sub plans once they are made. If you are out more than five days then let the substitute re-teach lessons; since there are no worksheets the final product will always be a different result.

Figure 5.1
Cover Page for Substitute Lesson Plans

SUBSTITUTE PLANS

Thank you for substituting for me today. Your time and help are greatly appreciated. The paper needed for today's lesson activities can be found on the right-hand corner of my desk in the organized paper trays. In case any of the planned activities do not take the entire time allotted, feel free to read to the students from our classroom library.

* If you need any assistance you may rely on the following trustworthy students:

Morning Tasks and Procedures:

Attendance:

Tardy Students:

Lunch Count:

Special Duties or Instructions:

Figure 5.2
Format for Substitute Plans

<u>Substitute Plans</u>
Schedule for Lesson Plans:

Time: _____ to _____
Subject:
Lesson Plan:

Time: _____ to _____
Subject:
Lesson Plan:

Time: _____ to _____
Subject:
Lesson Plan:

Time: _____ to _____
Lunch

Time: _____ to _____
Recess
Special Instructions:

Time: _____ to _____
Subject:
Lesson Plan:

Time: _____ to _____
Subject:
Lesson Plan:

Time: _____ to _____
Special Area Class
Students know the scheduled special and the location.

Time: _____ to _____
Clean Up, Pack Up, and Dismissal
Special Instructions:

Figure 5.3
Primary Substitute Lessons/Day 1

Subject: *Shared Reading/Main Idea*
Lesson Plan
• Choose a fictional book from our classroom library. • Students should predict what the story will be about by analyzing the title and illustrations on the cover. • Read the story out loud to the students.
• After reading, check predictions by asking: Were our predictions right about the story events? What happened in the beginning, middle, and end of the story? What was this story all about, or what was the main idea? • Write these words on the board: The story was about... • Tell students that they will tell what the story was all about by writing words or sentences and drawing a picture. Distribute a blank sheet of paper to each student. • Give sufficient time for students to complete the activity. Call on volunteers to share what they wrote and drew.

Subject: *Reading*
Lesson Plan
• Tell the students that we will practice our reading skills differently today by independently reading and reading with a partner or "buddy reading." • Ask students to take out their reading books, or to tell you where the reading books have been placed and distribute them. • Say: Choose a story from your reading book. Now don't read yet, let's talk about our reading strategies, what do good readers do? • After discussing reading strategies, say: Begin reading your story. Early finishers need to re-read. • Say: Okay, you have had a chance to practice reading, now it is time to read to a partner by "buddy reading" (group the students in twos). • Say: We're going to read by taking turns. The person in each group with the shortest hair will go first. • Tell early finishers to re-read to one another. Once everyone has finished taking their reading turn, repeat the procedure by letting them read with a partner of choice. • If there is still reading time remaining, select students to work together in centers (two per center) and let the remaining students work in their journals or choose a book from our class library.

Subject: *Writing*
Lesson Plan
• Read the alphabet with the students. • Hold a class discussion on what good writers do (space between words, form letters correctly, write neatly, use the lines appropriately). • Tell students that they are going to practice writing the alphabet—both capital and lower case letters. • Pass out lined paper and students should take out a pencil and an eraser. • Monitor the student's neatness. • Early finishers should write word wall words on the back.

Subject: *Phonics*
Lesson Plan
• Play I spy with the alphabet strip. "I spy a letter that makes the sound of ___. Which letter is it?" Let the students guess the answer and then continue the game several more times with you as the spy and then give the students a turn at being the spy. • Tell the students to take out their journals. • Choose a letter from the alphabet and tell students to write as many words as they can that begin with that letter sound. They can use words from around the room and textbooks to help them generate words. • Check to see who found the most words. • If time remains, play again with new letters.

Subject: *Social Studies/Manners*
Lesson Plan
• Identify and talk about the importance of the class rules. • Discuss what it means to be respectful (nice, considerate, taking turns, being polite, giving compliments). • Have students role play acts of respect.
• Distribute lined paper and tell students to draw and label an act of respect or one class rule that they followed today.

Subject: *Math/Sorting*
Lesson Plan
• Discuss what it means to sort objects (to group like and unlike attributes). • Call on students to stand at the front of the room that are alike in some way and have the other students guess your sorting rule (all wearing red, all have on sneakers). • Give several volunteers a turn to make like groups of students as the other students try to figure out their sorting rule. • Tell students to sort items from their pencil box. Tell students to guess how the person sitting next to them sorted. • Repeat by having students sort their pencil box items a different way. • Distribute blank paper and direct students to record how they sorted by titling their paper My Sorting Rule (write this on the board) and drawing three large circles on their paper. • Inside each circle direct students to draw and label how they sorted in three different ways. • Let students share how they sorted with the class. • Complete calendar activities if time allows (students know the routine).

Figure 5.3
Primary Substitute Lessons/Day 2

Subject: *Shared Reading*
Lesson Plan
• Choose a fictional book from our classroom library. • Discuss the definition of story characters (who the story is all about).
• Let students predict who the story might be about and what might happen to the character in the story by analyzing the picture on the cover of the book. • Read the story out loud to the students. • Check predictions that they made about the characters by asking: "Were our predictions right about the characters? Who can describe the characters? Why do you think the author wrote this story about these characters?" • Write these words on the board: The main characters were... • Tell students that they will tell who the main characters were in the story by drawing and labeling. • Call on volunteers to share their pictures.

Subject: *Reading*
Lesson Plan
• Tell the students that we will practice our reading skills differently today by independently reading and reading with a partner or buddy reading. • Ask students to take out their reading books, or to tell you where the reading books have been placed and distribute them. • Say: Choose a story from your reading book. Now don't read yet, let's talk about our reading strategies, what do good readers do? • After discussing reading strategies, say: Begin reading your story. Early finishers need to re-read. • Say: Okay, you have had a chance to practice reading, now it is time to read to a partner by "buddy reading" (group the students in twos). • Say: We're going to read by taking turns. The person in each group with the shortest hair will go first. • Tell early finishers to re-read to one another. Once everyone has finished taking their reading turn, repeat the procedure by letting them read with a partner of choice. • If there is still reading time remaining, select students to work together in centers (two per center) and let the remaining students work in their journals or choose a book from our class library.

Subject: *Writing*
Lesson Plan
• Tell the students that we will write an autobiography today. • Explain what an autobiography is (when a person writes facts about themselves). • Have students share interesting facts about themselves. • List some of those facts on the board.
• Distribute lined paper to the students and ask them to write a list of five words that describe them. • Direct students to use that list to help them write a paragraph about themselves. • Early finishers can draw a picture of themselves. • Give students the opportunity to share their work.

Subject: *Phonics*
Lesson Plan
• Play I spy with the alphabet strip. "I spy a letter that makes the sound of ___. Which letter is it?" Let the students guess the answer and then continue the game several more times with you as the spy and then give the students a turn at being the spy.
• Tell the students to take out their journals. • Choose a letter from the alphabet and tell students to write as many words as they can that begin with that letter sound. They can use words from around the room and textbooks to help them generate words. • Check to see who found the most words. • If time remains, play again with new letters.

Subject: *Social Studies/Playground Rules*
Lesson Plan
• Identify and discuss the purpose of playground rules. • Have students role play using playground rules. • Distribute lined paper and tell students to draw and label a playground rule.

Subject: *Math/Graphing*
Lesson Plan
• Discuss the purpose of graphs (tells information). • Vote on a class graph question, "What is your favorite _____?"
• Create a tally graph on the board with the students based on their favorite _____ (remind students what a bundle looks like). • Discuss the graph information: What do students like the most? ... and least? • Tell students that they are going to create their own graph using the class graph as a model. • After they create their graph on blank paper have them walk around and ask each other their graph question and instruct them to record the answers with a tally. • Let students share their results.
• Complete math calendar.

Figure 5.3
Primary Substitute Lessons/Day 3

Subject: *Shared Reading*
Lesson Plan
• Choose a fictional book from our classroom library. • Discuss the definition of story setting (where the story takes place).
• Let students predict where the story might take place by analyzing the picture on the cover of the book.
• Read the story out loud to the students. • Check predictions that they made about the setting by asking: "Were our predictions right about the setting of the story? Who can describe the setting? Why do you think the author chose this setting?" • Write these words on the board: The setting of the story is... • Tell students that they will tell the setting of the story by drawing and labeling. • Call on volunteers to share their pictures.

Subject: *Reading*
Lesson Plan
• Tell the students that we will practice our reading skills differently today by independently reading and reading with a partner or buddy reading. • Ask students to take out their reading books, or to tell you where the reading books have been placed and distribute them. • Say: Choose a story from your reading book. Now don't read yet, let's talk about our reading strategies, what do good readers do? • After discussing reading strategies, say: Begin reading your story. Early finishers need to re-read. • Say: Okay, you have had a chance to practice reading, now it is time to read to a partner by "buddy reading" (group the students in twos). • Say: We're going to read by taking turns. The person in each group with the shortest hair will go first. • Tell early finishers to re-read to one another. Once everyone has finished taking their reading turn, repeat the procedure by letting them read with a partner of choice. • If there is still reading time remaining, select students to work together in centers (two per center) and let the remaining students work in their journals or choose a book from our class library.

Subject: *Writing*
Lesson Plan
• Inform students that we will demonstrate appropriate writing skills by writing a letter. • Discuss the parts of a letter (date, greeting, body of the letter, closing, signature). • Let students help you write an example of a letter on the board. • Distribute lined paper and have students either copy our letter or write their own. • Monitor student neatness and help students with spelling questions.

Subject: *Phonics*
Lesson Plan
• Play I spy with the alphabet strip. "I spy a letter that makes the sound of ___. Which letter is it?" Let the students guess the answer and then continue the game several more times with you as the spy and then give the students a turn at being the spy.
• Tell the students to take out their journals. • Choose a letter from the alphabet and tell students to write as many words as they can that begin with that letter sound. They can use words from around the room and textbooks to help them generate words. • Check to see who found the most words. • If time remains, play again with new letters.

Subject: *Social Studies/Manners*
Lesson Plan
• Identify the lunch room rules and routines and discuss the importance of following them. • Discuss what it means to have manners (polite, taking turns, being patient, being respectful). • Have students role play acts of good manners.
• Distribute lined paper and tell students to draw and label what good manners mean to them.

Subject: *Math/Measurement*
Lesson Plan
• Discuss the terms: short, shortest, long, longest. • Call three random students to the front of the room. Have other students order them from shortest to longest. • Repeat with groups of four students, five students, and six students. • Tell students to choose three random items from their pencil box and ask them to order the items from shortest to longest. • Repeat by having students order groups of 4, 5, and 6 items from their pencil box. • Have students put everything back in their pencil box and switch pencil boxes with a partner. Have students repeat, but this time order longest to shortest with items in their friends' pencil boxes. • Distribute a blank piece of paper and have students draw four sticks from shortest to longest on the front and from longest to shortest on the back. Then ask students to label the shortest and longest stick that they drew on both sides.

Figure 5.3
Primary Substitute Lessons/Day 4

Subject: *Shared Reading*
Lesson Plan
• Choose a fictional book from our classroom library. • Discuss the definition of a story title (the name of the story).
• Let students analyze the title on the cover of the book by saying: "Let's predict why the author might have chosen this title."
• Read the story out loud to the students. • Discuss again why the author chose this setting and talk about different titles that the story could have. • Distribute blank paper to students. • Tell students that they will create a new title and cover for the story by writing and drawing. • Call on volunteers to share their ideas.

Subject: *Reading*
Lesson Plan
• Tell the students that we will practice our reading skills differently today by independently reading and reading with a partner or buddy reading. • Ask students to take out their reading books, or to tell you where the reading books have been placed and distribute them. • Say: Choose a story from your reading book. Now don't read yet, let's talk about our reading strategies, what do good readers do? • After discussing reading strategies, say: Begin reading your story. Early finishers need to re-read. • Say: Okay, you have had a chance to practice reading, now it is time to read to a partner by "buddy reading" (group the students in twos). • Say: We're going to read by taking turns. The person in each group with the shortest hair will go first. • Tell early finishers to re-read to one another. Once everyone has finished taking their reading turn, repeat the procedure by letting them read with a partner of choice. • If there is still reading time remaining, select students to work together in centers (two per center) and let the remaining students work in their journals or choose a book from our class library.

Subject: *Writing*
Lesson Plan
• Inform students that we will have fun with writing today by writing about any topic of choice and drawing a picture to match. • Distribute lined paper and have students begin their writing piece. • Monitor student neatness and help students with spelling questions.

Subject: *Phonics*
Lesson Plan
• Play I spy with the alphabet strip. "I spy a letter that makes the sound of ___. Which letter is it?" Let the students guess the answer and then continue the game several more times with you as the spy and then give the students a turn at being the spy.
• Tell the students to take out their journals. • Choose a letter from the alphabet and tell students to write as many words as they can that begin with that letter sound. They can use words from around the room and textbooks to help them generate words. • Check to see who found the most words. • If time remains, play again with new letters.

Subject: *Social Studies/Rules*
Lesson Plan
• Identify the routine for walking in line in the hallway and discuss the importance of following this routine (being quiet and respectful to other students who are learning while we're in the hallway). • Have students practice how to walk in the hallway.
• Distribute lined paper and tell students to draw and write about what a well-mannered line looks and sounds like.

Subject: *Math/Numbers to 20*
Lesson Plan
• Practice counting to 20 with the students. • Write the numbers 1-20 on the board but leave out a few select numbers. Allow volunteers to write the missing numbers. • Get 20 pieces of blank paper and write with a marker the numbers 1-20 with each number on its own sheet of paper. As you write the numbers talk about the proper formation of each number. • Mix up the numbers and distribute each number to a different student. • Have students order themselves in a line according to the correct number order 1-20. The students that don't have a number will check for accuracy and read the numbers once they are in order. • Collect the numbers and play around the world with them (two students at a time try to recognize the number and the first to identify it remains standing and goes against the next student to see who recognizes the next number shown first).
• Distribute lined paper and tell students to write the numbers 1-20 neatly. Remind them to space between each number.
• Early finishers can draw 20 objects on the back of their paper or be challenged to draw and label more. • Complete the calendar activities (students know the routine).

Figure 5.3
Primary Substitute Lessons/Day 5

Subject: *Shared Reading*
Lesson Plan
• Choose a fictional book from our classroom library. • Discuss the definition of a story title (the name of the story).
• Let students analyze the title on the cover of the book by saying: "Let's predict why the author might have chosen this title."
• Read the story out loud to the students. • Discuss again why the author chose this title and talk about different titles that the story could have. • Distribute blank paper to students. • Tell students that they will create a new title and cover for the story by writing and drawing. • Call on volunteers to share their ideas.

Subject: *Reading*
Lesson Plan
• Tell the students that we will practice our reading skills differently today by independently reading and reading with a partner or buddy reading. • Ask students to take out their reading books, or to tell you where the reading books have been placed and distribute them. • Say: Choose a story from your reading book. Now don't read yet, let's talk about our reading strategies, what do good readers do? • After discussing reading strategies, say: Begin reading your story. Early finishers need to re-read. • Say: Okay, you have had a chance to practice reading, now it is time to read to a partner by "buddy reading" (group the students in twos). • Say: We're going to read by taking turns. The person in each group with the shortest hair will go first. • Tell early finishers to re-read to one another. Once everyone has finished taking their reading turn, repeat the procedure by letting them read with a partner of choice. • If there is still reading time remaining, select students to work together in centers (two per center) and let the remaining students work in their journals or choose a book from our class library.

Subject: *Writing*
Lesson Plan
• Inform students that we will have fun with writing today by writing about any topic of choice and drawing a picture to match. • Distribute lined paper and have students begin their writing piece. • Monitor student neatness and help students with spelling questions.

Subject: *Phonics*
Lesson Plan
• Play I spy with the alphabet strip. "I spy a letter that makes the sound of _____. Which letter is it?" Let the students guess the answer and then continue the game several more times with you as the spy and then give the students a turn at being the spy. • Tell the students to take out their journals. • Choose a letter from the alphabet and tell students to write as many words as they can that begin with that letter sound. They can use words from around the room and textbooks to help them generate words. • Check to see who found the most words. • If time remains, play again with new letters.

Subject: *Social Studies/Feelings*
Lesson Plan
• Identify the different types of feelings that people experience. • Make a list of the different types of feelings that students give and have students give facial expressions that demonstrate these feelings. • Distribute lined paper and tell students to write and draw about the feelings that they experience today.

Subject: *Math/Addition*
Lesson Plan
• Identify what the signs + and = mean by writing them on the board and discussing them. • Demonstrate addition stories by calling random groups of students to the front of the room. (If two girls and two boys were on a bench, how many students were on the bench all together?) Give several examples. • Write five random addition problems on the board and ask students to solve the problems in their journal. • Have volunteers solve the problems on the board while the rest of the students check their answers. • Have students create ten addition problems of their own in their journals. Then instruct students to exchange journals in order to solve each other's addition problems. • Next have students return the journals so they may check their partner's work. • Complete the calendar activities (students know the routine).

Figure 5.4
Intermediate Substitute Lessons/Day 1

Subject: *Reading*
Lesson Plan
• Let students choose a book to read from our classroom library. • Review the reading strategies with the students.
• Tell the students that they will have twenty minutes of sustained silent reading time. • At the end of the twenty minutes do a book talk by allowing students to share what they read (talk time should be under three minutes each).
• After the book talk, instruct students to write interview questions for the author or a character from the story.

Subject: *Writing*
Lesson Plan
• Conduct a class discussion on what the students are good at doing (riding bike, skating, making a bracelet). • Today you will explain in writing how to do something. You will include a title, materials needed, and directions in a step-by-step list or paragraph format. • Write transition words on the board and review with students: first, second, third, next, then, lastly, and finally. • Let the students share.

Subject: *Math*
Lesson Plan
• Today we will solve two-digit addition problems. • Write five two-digit addition problems on the board. • Instruct the students to solve the addition problems in their math journals. • Check the answers with the students and discuss strategies they used. • Conduct a relay race with students by making two teams and writing two-digit addition problems on the board. Students should all try to figure out the answer in their journal. The first team with the correct answer wins. Repeat until you feel necessary to stop. • Pass out paper and instruct students to write twenty two-digit addition problems for another student to solve. • Give students time to complete this assignment. • Next, tell students to switch papers with someone else and try to solve their friend's addition problems. • Direct the students to switch papers once they have completed each problem.
• Instruct the original creator of the addition problems to check their friend's work.

Subject: *Social Studies*
Lesson Plan
• Ask the students: "Who watches the news and what is it about?" Talk with the students and identify the importance of watching the news (to inform us about what's going on around the world). • Discuss recent topics that students have seen on the news (sports, weather, current events). • Instruct students to work with partners to create a news report about sports, weather, or a current event that will be shared with the rest of the class in a mock news broadcast. • Give students time to write and share.

Figure 5.4
Intermediate Substitute Lessons/Day 2

Subject: *Reading*
Lesson Plan
• Let students choose a book to read from our classroom library. • Review the reading strategies with the students.
• Tell the students that they will have twenty minutes of sustained silent reading time. • At the end of the twenty minutes do a book talk by allowing students to share what they read (talk time should be under three minutes each).
• After the book talk, instruct students to write a paragraph about the main idea or story events.

Subject: *Writing*
Lesson Plan
• Today you will write a friendly letter. • Hold a class discussion on the friendly letter format: date, greeting, body, closing, signature. • Write a friendly letter on the board with the class to show as a model. • Pass out lined paper and instruct students to write a friendly letter by using the model as a guide.

Subject: *Math*
Lesson Plan
• Today we will solve subtraction problems. • Write five subtraction problems on the board. • Instruct the students to solve the subtraction problems in their math journals. • Check the answers with the students and discuss strategies they used. • Conduct a relay race with students by making two teams and writing subtraction problems on the board. Students should all try to figure out the answer in their journal. The first team with the correct answer wins. Repeat until you feel necessary to stop.
• Pass out paper and instruct students to write twenty subtraction problems for another student to solve. • Give students time to complete this assignment. • Next, tell students to switch papers with someone else and try to solve their friend's subtraction problems. • Direct the students to switch papers once they have completed each problem. • Instruct the original creator of the subtraction problems to check their friend's work.

Subject: *Social Studies*
Lesson Plan
• Today we will describe similarities and differences between people. Create a Venn diagram in front of the class and work with the students to compare two students. Write the similarities in the center of the Venn diagram and the differences in the left and right areas of the Venn diagram. • Pass out paper and have students create their own Venn diagram comparing themselves to someone else in the class. • Provide time for students to share their work.

Figure 5.4
Intermediate Substitute Lessons/Day 3

Subject: *Reading*
Lesson Plan
• Let students choose a book to read from our classroom library. • Review the reading strategies with the students.
• Tell the students that they will have twenty minutes of sustained silent reading time. • At the end of the twenty minutes do a book talk by allowing students to share what they read (talk time should be under three minutes each).
• After the book talk, instruct students to rewrite the ending to the story. Allow students to share the original ending and the new ending that they created.

Subject: *Writing*
Lesson Plan
• Today we will write a story based on personal experience. • Hold a class discussion on the format of a good story and record the format on the board: title, topic sentence, beginning events, middle events, end events, characters, and setting. • Instruct students to use this format to write a short story based on a personal experience. Pass out lined paper and instruct students to begin writing their stories. • Provide time for students to share their stories.

Subject: *Math*
Lesson Plan
• Today we will solve subtraction problems. • Write five subtraction problems on the board. • Instruct the students to solve the subtraction problems in their math journals. • Check the answers with the students and discuss strategies they used. • Conduct a relay race with students by making two teams and writing subtraction problems on the board. Students should all try to figure out the answer in their journal. The first team with the correct answer wins. Repeat until you feel necessary to stop. • Pass out paper and instruct students to write twenty subtraction problems for another student to solve. • Give students time to complete this assignment. • Next, tell students to switch papers with someone else and try to solve their friend's subtraction problems. • Direct the students to switch papers once they have completed each problem. • Instruct the original creator of the subtraction problems to check their friend's work.

Subject: *Social Studies*
Lesson Plan
• Today we will identify ways we can make a difference and help preserve the earth. • Discuss the importance of recycling and conserving energy. • Pass out blank paper and tell students to create a poster to get more people involved in saving the earth. Their poster should include three ways people can contribute to helping our earth stay healthy. • Provide time for students to share their work.

Figure 5.4
Intermediate Substitute Lessons/Day 4

Subject: *Reading*
Lesson Plan
• Let students choose a book to read from our classroom library. • Review the reading strategies with the students.
• Tell the students that they will have twenty minutes of sustained silent reading time. • At the end of the twenty minutes do a book talk by allowing students to share what they read (talk time should be under three minutes each).
• After the book talk, instruct students to write a friendly letter to the author telling him or her how they felt about the book, their favorite part of the book, and what they liked about the illustrations, main characters, or the main idea.
• Provide time for students to share their work.

Subject: *Writing*
Lesson Plan
• Today we will write a skit with a partner and perform the skits. • Conduct a class discussion on what a skit is (an event or story acted out by people) and discuss how the dialogue is written for a skit (write the name of the character speaking and the text of what each character says with quotation marks). • Create a short skit with students by writing on the board. • Instruct students to work with partners to create a skit involving a problem and solution. • Provide time for students to perform their skit.

Subject: *Math*
Lesson Plan
• Today we will solve multiplication problems. • Write five multiplication problems on the board. • Instruct the students to solve the multiplication problems in their math journals. • Check the answers with the students and discuss strategies they used. • Conduct a relay race with students by making two teams and writing multiplication problems on the board. Students should all try to figure out the answer in their journal. The first team with the correct answer wins. Repeat until you feel necessary to stop. • Pass out paper and instruct students to write twenty multiplication problems for another student to solve.
• Give students time to complete this assignment. • Next, tell students to switch papers with someone else and try to solve their friend's multiplication problems. • Direct the students to switch papers once they have completed each problem.
• Instruct the original creator of the multiplication problems to check their friend's work.

Subject: *Social Studies*
Lesson Plan
• Discuss the reasons why we have laws in our country (to maintain order and safety). • List laws that students are familiar with. • Pass out lined paper and ask students to imagine that they are the president of the United States and they need to establish five new laws and explain why our country needs these laws. • Provide time for students to share their thoughts with the class.

Figure 5.4
Intermediate Substitute Lessons/Day 5

Subject: *Reading*
Lesson Plan
• Let students choose a book to read from our classroom library. • Review the reading strategies with the students.
• Tell the students that they will have twenty minutes of sustained silent reading time. • At the end of the twenty minutes do a book talk by allowing students to share what they read (talk time should be under three minutes each).
• After the book talk, instruct students to imagine that they are the author of the story and to give the story a new title and illustrate a new book jacket. • Provide time for students to share.

Subject: *Writing*
Lesson Plan
• Today we will write a poem on any topic. • Hold a class discussion on characteristics of poems (tells feelings, describes something, sometimes rhymes). • Create a poem with the students and record it on the board. • Instruct the students to create a poem on a topic of their choice and to also add an illustration. • Provide time for students to share their poems.

Subject: *Math*
Lesson Plan
• Today we will solve division problems. • Write five division problems on the board. • Instruct the students to solve the division problems in their math journals. • Check the answers with the students and discuss strategies they used. • Conduct a relay race with students by making two teams and writing division problems on the board. Students should all try to figure out the answer in their journal. The first team with the correct answer wins. Repeat until you feel necessary to stop. • Pass out paper and instruct students to write twenty division problems for another student to solve. • Give students time to complete this assignment. • Next, tell students to switch papers with someone else and try to solve their friend's division problems.
• Direct the students to switch papers once they have completed each problem. • Instruct the original creator of the division problems to check their friend's work.

Subject: *Social Studies*
Lesson Plan
• Discuss the importance of having a job (to make money in order to afford a home, food, and clothing). • Talk about different careers and what their parents do for a living. • Discuss what students want to be when they grow up.
• Distribute lined paper and instruct students to write a paragraph about one of the following: the career they want to pursue as an adult and why, or their parent's career and job responsibilities. • Provide time for students to share what they wrote.

Chapter 6
Ready Made Plans for the First Week of School

You are at the two-week mark before the school year officially begins and you may start to feel so overwhelmed with things to do and prepare for that you probably can't even decide on where to start. Use this chapter's helpful checklists and ready made plans as you prepare for the first week of school.

Task Checklist
Ten Days Prior to School

☐ Obtain your class list along with addresses and send your students a postcard greeting. On the postcard introduce yourself, mention how excited you are about meeting them on the first day of school, and tell them that you have planned exciting activities for learning that are full of fun and exploration. ★**Tip:** Use the school's address as your return address.

☐ Time to take inventory and purchase any teaching supplies that your school has not provided for you. Reference the following necessities list for ideas:

Teaching Tools:

_sentence strips	_transparencies	_pocket charts	_CD of symphony music
_chart paper	_dry erase board	_a pointer	_easel
_radio	_yardstick	_prize box	_recess equipment
_prize box/prizes	_sponges	_small bucket	_clothespins
_flashlight	_rocking chair	_recess games (outdoor and indoor)	

Arts & Craft Stuff:

_construction paper	_pipe cleaners	_yarn	_wiggly eyes
_feathers	_assorted buttons	_beads	_finger paint
_paint	_paint brushes	_glitter	_assorted fabric squares
_clay	_sand	_cotton balls	_cotton swabs
_craft sticks	_pom-poms	_sandwich baggies	_quart size baggies
_brown paper bags	_wax paper	_tin foil	_paper cups/plates

☐ Purchase special pencils, erasers, and pencil grips to place on each student's desk for the first day of school. Sharpen the pencils so they are ready to use.

Task Checklist
Nine Days Prior to School

☐ Sketch your classroom layout, set up your classroom, and organize your desk (refer to ch.1).

☐ Design a word or vocabulary wall (refer to ch.2).

☐ Decide on and design classroom bulletin boards around your classroom and, if applicable, in the hall (refer to ch.2).

☐ Hang all displays that are required by your school or grade level, such as the alphabet, number line, color words, reading strategies, and writing process.

Task Checklist
Eight Days Prior to School

☐ Set up subject bins in order to have an established area for organizing materials needed for teaching lessons on a daily basis (refer to ch.3).

☐ Early childhood teachers should set up theme bins to organize monthly activities, decorations, and center materials (refer to ch.3).

☐ Organize math manipulatives (refer to ch.3).

☐ Label the classroom doors and drawers for efficient organization of everyday supplies (refer to ch.3).

Task Checklist
Seven Days Prior to School

☐ Write your long range plan (refer to ch.3).

☐ Give a copy of the long range plans that you have written to your principal.

Task Checklist
Six Days Prior to School

☐ Write your emergency substitute plans (refer to ch.5).

☐ Find out where your school would like you to store your emergency substitute plans and place them in that area.

Task Checklist
Five Days Prior to School

☐ Know the fire drill route for your class and hang a clipboard with a class roster by all exits in the room. You will need to take this roster with you each time you leave the building due to emergencies.

☐ Make student name tags if you plan to have students wear them for the first few days of school.

☐ Create a seating chart and place laminated name tags on the desks or tables. Velcro or clear packing tape is suggested for mounting name tags to desktops.

☐ Secure laminated name tags to the lockers or cubbies.

☐ Plan and display the daily class schedule (refer to ch.1).

Task Checklist
Four Days Prior to School

☐ Establish a sign-out system to keep track of where your students are at all times of the day (refer to ch.1).

☐ Design a class behavior chart and post it in a visible area (refer to ch.7).

☐ Create a student job chart and assign jobs for the first week of school (refer to ch.1).

☐ Display the center chart which will assign or allow students to choose their daily center (refer to ch.9). Establish an area for this display even though centers won't begin until you are ready.

Task Checklist
Three Days Prior to School

☐ Put together a classroom first aid kit containing gloves, band aids, gauze, nurse passes, a pen, and a flashlight.

☐ Establish and organize student portfolios in alphabetical order. You may want to consider a portable file holder so that you can transport the portfolios to meetings.

☐ Retrieve the required student textbooks from the school book closet.

☐ Visit the school library and choose an age-appropriate *back-to-school* and *following class rules* book to read to the students. Read chapter seven to prepare for teaching the class rules.

☐ Type a list of your car riders/walkers and group the bus riders according to the bus they ride. Post this list in a visible spot and always take the list with you when walking the bus riders out to their bus.

☐ Pre-print sticker labels if you plan to label any of the student's folders or journals according to subjects or use, such as Homework Folder, Math Journal, Morning Journal, Spelling Folder.

☐ Write a welcome letter to be distributed on the first day of school. Attach a copy of the long range plan and a student supply list. Include the following when writing the welcome letter:

– teacher bio	– the school phone number	– your professional E-mail
– the class schedule	– schedule of specials	– class rules
– volunteer information	– homework information	– arrival and dismissal times

☐ Copy the student information sheet which needs to be completed by the parents (see figure 6.1).

☐ Inquire about the times that teachers need to arrive and can leave the school building and the times when students will arrive and are dismissed.

☐ Get familiar with the school grounds and the procedure for the signing in, lunch count, attendance cards, tardy students, sending students to the nurse and office, and emergency procedures.

☐ Review your students' folders from the previous year so that you are aware of any student issues or concerns. Get familiar with all IEP requirements that you are responsible for implementing. See an administrator if you have any questions.

Task Checklist
Two Days Prior to School

☐ Write lesson plans, make copies of activities, and get teaching materials ready for the first week of school (see figures 6.2 and 6.3 for examples).

☐ Display objectives (refer to ch. 1).

☐ Decide on a morning work activity for the first day of school (coloring sheet, story paper, crossword puzzle) and make copies for the students.

☐ On chart paper create a morning directions poster explaining what to do as the students come in the room.

☐ Create an icebreaker such as a name puzzle to help students get to know each other. To create a name puzzle:

    1. Cut a large piece of poster board into interconnecting puzzle pieces (make one puzzle piece for each student).

    2. Laminate the pieces and write a student's name on each piece. Since the puzzle is laminated you can erase the names and reuse the name puzzle year after year.

    3. Find a bean bag or beach ball to help with this activity (see figure 6.2).

Task Checklist
One Day Prior to School

☐ Set up a radio to play a music CD that contains soft orchestra music to relax students as they enter the classroom and begin their morning work.

☐ Check your professional E-mail.

☐ Most likely you will be expected to attend meetings today.

☐ Tie up any loose ends by completing unfinished tasks.

☐ Get a good night's rest.

☐ Relax, everything will be great!

Figure 6.1
Student Information Sheet

STUDENT INFORMATION SHEET

Child's Name: _____

Child's Nickname: _____

Child's Birthday: _____

Guardian's Names: _____

Home Phone Number: _____

Work or Cell Phone Number: _____

Does your child have any allergies? _____

Do you have any concerns? _____

May your child have his or her picture taken? _____

What are your child's strengths? _____

What are your child's challenges? _____

Do you allow your child to partake in parties/celebrations?   ☐ Yes   ☐ No

If not, be specific:

_____

_____

_____

Any other important information that you feel the teacher should be aware of?

_____

_____

_____

Plans for the First Day of School

Understand that the first day of school will not adhere to your typical daily class schedule. Instead, make plans for every thirty-minute time block during the day that revolves around the students getting to know the teacher, each other, the school, the rules, and the routines.

Figure 6.2

LESSON PLANS FOR THE FIRST DAY OF SCHOOL

Before the students arrive:
- Sign in and check your faculty mailbox for the attendance cards.
- Distribute the welcome pencils.
- Place an easy or open-ended activity on each student's desk for morning work.
  (coloring sheet, writing paper with a writing prompt, crossword puzzle, etc.)
- Play soft symphony music in the background to welcome students.
- Post the morning directions poster on the chalkboard.

9:00
The school bell will ring.

9:00-9:10
Greet students at the door with a smile. Have students place their book bags on the backs of their chairs. The only thing they should need is the pencil that the teacher has provided for each student and maybe their crayons. Direct the student's attention to the morning directions poster and morning work.

9:10-9:30
Students will continue morning work and listen to the announcements. Explain the morning work routine that you would like to establish. Take attendance and the lunch count information. Explain the job chart and send the messengers to the office with the attendance cards.

9:30-10:15
Read a *back-to-school* book. In whole group have students create a web about the emotions they are feeling as they begin school this year. Let students express their feelings on paper through drawing and writing. Give students a chance to talk about what they wrote in small groups. Collect this writing piece and later date and place it in student portfolios to serve as a benchmark for their writing abilities at the beginning of the year.

10:15-10:45
Students will empty their book bags and we will collect the necessary supplies (tissues, baggies, etc.) and put them in the appropriate place. Help students organize their personal supplies and label their journals and folders according to their uses. Distribute assigned books and demonstrate how to put on the book covers. Go over the proper uses for the supplies and books.

10:45-11:15
Now that the book bags are empty, explain the locker or cubby procedures and practice.

Figure 6.2 continued

LESSON PLANS FOR THE FIRST DAY OF SCHOOL
Continued

11:15-11:45
Tour the classroom and the school. Practice how to line up and walk in the hallway appropriately (refer to ch.8 on how to manage *the line)*. Explain the sign-out, bathroom, drink, and lunch procedures.

11:45-12:30
Getting to Know You Game
Have students sit in a circle as you get a bean bag or beach ball ready. Explain to the students that we are going to get to know each other by playing a listening game.
Explain the directions:
-We will toss the bean bag (or beach ball) and the one who catches it will tell us their name.
-You must pay attention and listen because you can't pass the bean bag to someone
  who has already told us their name.
-Whoever catches the bean bag must say, "My name is _____." And then everyone
  else replies, "Nice to meet you _____." Continue until everyone has had a turn.
- Pass out the name puzzle pieces. Explain that we will work as a team to put the
  name puzzle together.

12:30-1:00
Lunch/Introduce the lunchroom rules and procedures.

1:00-1:45
Recess
Explain the playground rules. If possible, provide for a slightly longer recess so students may get to know one another and begin to form friendships.

1:45-2:20
Establishing Class Rules Activity
- Read a story on the topic of class rules.
- Discuss the story events and the importance of rules.
- Create a class rules poster with the students.
- Read the rules aloud with the students.
- Have the students sign their names at the bottom of the poster demonstrating that they agree
  to follow the class rules.
- Distribute your school's policy handbook to be signed by students and parents at home.

2:20-3:00
Specials

3:00-3:15
Pass out important papers (welcome letter, student information sheet, student supply list, etc.).

3:15-3:30
Explain clean-up and pack-up procedure. Prepare to go home. Organize the students in line according to walkers and buses. Take bus list with you to help students find their appropriate bus.

Plans for the Second Day of School

On the second day of school begin the normal daily schedule that you are going to implement throughout the year. Although you are following the appropriate schedule, the second day activities will still not yet reflect normal everyday lesson plans. Your day will consist mostly of reinforcing procedures that were taught yesterday, giving pre-assessments to see what your students know and explaining the homework expectations. See figure 6.3 for an example of second day of school activities.

Figure 6.3

SECOND DAY OF SCHOOL LESSON PLANS

9:00-9:10
School bell will ring. Greet students as they enter the room. Monitor students as they begin the morning procedures independently.

9:10-9:30
Listen to the morning announcements, take attendance and lunch count. Go over the jobs assigned on the job chart. Review the morning procedure with the entire class. Give praise to those who did a great job following the morning procedures.

9:30-10:15
Reading Block
Begin running records by testing 6-8 students per day (refer to ch.9 for more information on administering running records). While you are performing running records with one student at a time, assign the rest of the class an activity for each passing fifteen minutes to half hour. Activities for students could be reading and writing a reflection, following written directions to perform a task, or making a book. Do not score the running records until a later time. ★Tip: Since students just completed activities that required a lot of sitting, provide a stretch break or guide students through a wiggle work-out (stretching exercises).

10:15-11:00
Have students complete any writing benchmark tests that are necessary. If you have extra time, discuss the role of the school nurse, what constitutes a visit to the nurse, and visit the nurse's office.

11:00-11:40
Phonics, Word Wall, or Spelling
Follow the phonics curriculum guide and complete the first lesson, complete word wall activities, or begin spelling lessons.

11:40-12:30
Writing Block
Follow the writing curriculum guide and complete the first lesson. Explain the routine and purpose for student-teacher conferencing on writing skills. Tell students that you will meet with a few students each day to hold goals conferences. Begin the routine and writing portfolios today by meeting with one student to discuss writing abilities and set goals while the other students complete their assigned writing activity.

12:30-1:00
Lunch/Review lunchroom rules and procedures.

Figure 6.3 continued

SECOND DAY OF SCHOOL LESSON PLANS
Continued

1:00-1:30
Recess
Have students identify playground rules and safety.

1:30-2:20
Math Block
Explain and distribute the math pre-assessment for students to complete in order to assess what the students know and can do. The math pre-assessment will more than likely take less than forty minutes to complete. If there is extra time in the math block, practice the emergency procedures for reacting during a fire drill.

2:20-3:00
Specials

3:00-3:15
Social Studies
Introduce the social studies unit by reading a book on the first focus skill scheduled to be taught. Create a KWL chart to begin the unit.

3:15-3:30
Explain homework procedure, assign homework, clean up, and pack up to go home.

Plans for the Third Day of School

The third day will follow the normal schedule and curriculum lesson plans with the exception of reading. Continue to administer running records during the reading block and introduce DEAR time or SSR and practice. You will also find yourself repeating the directions for the routines and procedures throughout the day—this is to be expected.

Plans for the Fourth and Fifth Days of School

The fourth and fifth days will also follow the normal schedule and curriculum with the exception of reading instruction. Focus on completing running records so that you can begin grouping the children into diagnostic reading groups. The last two days of the first week of school are exciting because you will begin teaching the routine for reading groups, seatwork, and center activities. The main challenges facing you for the next few weeks will be training students on the reading group rotation procedure (see ch.9), preparing students for being independent workers, and teaching students how to properly use the center activities. Remember to hold high expectations for center and seatwork activities if you want students to be productive. ★**Tip:** Introduce centers one at a time to the entire class. Model and discuss how to use and clean up each center appropriately and explain the consequences for misbehavior. Every time a new center is added to the classroom, the teacher must post and read the written directions and also model how to properly use the center.

Chapter 7
Behavior Management Strategies

Chapter seven will share ways to prevent discipline problems by implementing tried-and-true behavior management strategies, giving students ownership of the classroom rules, providing a variety of behavior management charts that are ready to use in the classroom, and giving tips on ways to involve parents.

Establishing Classroom Rules

To help the students *buy into* the classroom rules they must first have ownership of them. Even though students are involved in the process, the teacher should decide ahead of time what the final set of rules will be. ★**Tip:** The secret for giving student ownership is to guide them toward stating the rules you would like established along with listing the ideas that students come up with independently and then choose the generated rules that reflect what is most important for your classroom environment. See figure 7.1 for examples of appropriate classroom rules. Techniques for establishing your classroom rules:

1. School rules must be established on the first day of school. It is important not to establish more than five rules so that students can remember and refer to them easily.

2. Read a story to the students about a fictitious character who deals with consequences because he/she chooses not to follow school rules.

3. Discuss the importance of school rules (rules keep us safe, help keep us focused, enable us to learn, etc.).

4. Explain to the students that this is their classroom and it is their job to make the classroom rules.

5. Let the students brainstorm a list of rules they would establish for the class. List those ideas on a class chart.

6. Have students vote on a title for the rules (*School Rules Are Cool, Our Class Rules*).

7. Write a formal classroom rules poster with the class. As the teacher, you already know the rules you would like in place. Choose the students' rules that match what you had in mind.

8. Read the final set of rules aloud with the students.

9. You may choose to have the students discuss or role play expected behaviors for each rule.

10. Post the rules in a visible area within the classroom. Primary teachers may choose to add picture clues for each rule.

11. Remind students of the rules as necessary so they don't forget their existence and importance, however do not dwell or reiterate the rules to a point of exhaustion.

Figure 7.1a
Primary Classroom Rules

Our Class Rules

1. We will be respectful.

2. We will take turns speaking.

3. We will not bring toys to school.

4. We will share.

5. We will work and play safely.

Figure 7.1b
Primary Classroom Rules

School Rules Are Cool

1. Choose to use indoor voices inside the school.

2. Choose to walk in the classroom and hallway.

3. Choose to raise your hand to speak.

4. Choose to keep our classroom clean.

5. Choose to keep your hands and feet to yourself.

Figure 7.1c
Intermediate Classroom Rules

Student Responsibilities

1. I am responsible for being respectful to myself, others, and school property.

2. I am responsible for following the directions.

3. I am responsible for my work area.

4. I am responsible for my learning.

5. I am responsible for doing my best.

Figure 7.1d
Intermediate Classroom Rules

Class Pledge

I promise to...

1. Complete my work on time.

2. Raise my hand to speak.

3. Listen to the speaker.

4. Be respectful in the halls and bathroom.

5. Be kind to others and mind my own business.

Explaining the Classroom Rules to Parents

It is very important to familiarize parents with your class rules and consequences by sending home a parent information letter. See figure 7.2 for an example of a letter which communicates class rules and expectations to parents.

Figure 7.2
Example Parent Letter Explaining Class Rules and Expectations

Behavior Management Information

Dear Parents,

Today our class discussed the importance of having class rules. We came to the consensus that rules keep us safe and help motivate us to learn and work at our very best. With this in mind, the students collaborated to establish our classroom rules. The following five rules were chosen:

OUR CLASSROOM RULES

1. We will keep our hands and feet to ourselves.
2. We will raise our hand to speak.
3. We will listen to the speaker.
4. We will complete our work on time.
5. We will always do our best.

All students are guaranteed the right to learn in a safe environment. Our class rules will be implemented through a *behavior stop light chart*. The following consequences have been established to maintain our class rules:

• Each child's name has been placed on a clothespin and clipped to the behavior chart that is in the form of a stop light. All students begin each day on the green light.

• If a student chooses to break one of the rules they will move their clothespin up to the yellow light which is a verbal warning.

• A student which breaks the rules a second time will then move their clothespin up to the red light—which requires the student to serve a time out or ten minutes off of their recess time. During a timeout, a teacher-student conference will be held about his or her behavior choices.

• Students who break the rules a third time will have a note sent home to their parents which will explain the rules that were broken for the day. The note will need to be signed by the parent and returned the following day.

• Most, if not all, behavior issues will be handled by the teacher. Depending on the severity of the behavior, the principal and/or vice principal can and may be involved.

I look forward to all of the students beginning the year in a positive manner. If you have any questions, please do not hesitate to call.

Thank You,

(teacher's name)

Class Behavior Modification Charts

To implement the class rules you will need to maintain a class behavior modification chart. The following are behavior modification charts that will reinforce the student's responsibility for their actions.

The Stop Light

The purpose of this behavior modification device is to have students move the clothespin with their name on it each time they are not following the rules. Each time a student moves their clothespin they have a consequence.

Steps for making the behavior stop light:

1. Create a stop light by cutting a large white poster board to the size of 46″l x 24″w.

2. Add a large green, yellow, and red circle to the white poster board.

3. Buy a bag of clothespins and write each student's name on his or her own clothespin.

4. Secure the stop light in a visible area, preferably in the front of the room.

5. Place the clothespins at the bottom of the stop light so that they are all clipped next to the green light.

6. Each time a student moves their clip they have a consequence.

    — Green light: Good Behavior

    — Yellow light: Verbal Warning

    — Red light: Loss of Five Minutes from Recess and Parent Contact

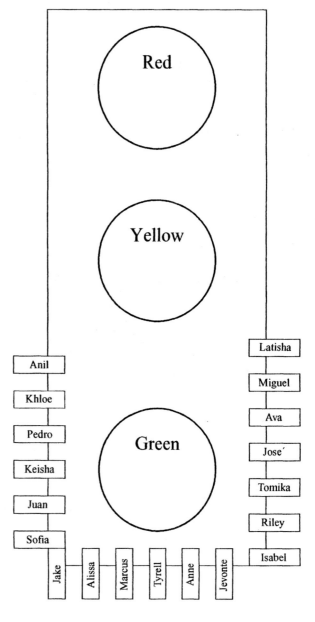

Behavior Cards

The object of this chart is to have students move their behavior card each time they are not following the rules. Each time a student moves their card they have a consequence.

How to set up a chart for behavior cards:

- Place a large pocket chart at the front of the room.
- In the top pocket place a sentence strip stating: *I am following the rules.*
- Under this sentence strip place index cards in a vertical position bearing each of the student's names.
- In the next available pocket place a sentence strip that states: *I am following some of the rules.*
- Count two more pockets down and place a sentence strip in this pocket that states: *I am not following the rules.*
- Each time a student moves their card under a sentence strip they have a consequence.

    — I am following the rules: Demonstrating Good Behavior

    — I am following some of the rules: Verbal Warning

    — I am not following the rules: Loss of Ten Minutes from Recess and Parent Contact

---

Class Behavior Chart

I am following the rules.

Alissa	Marcus	Isabel	Jake	Tamika	Riley	Tyrell
Khloe	Juan	Sofia	Keisha	Pedro	Anne	Dwayne

I am following some of the rules.

I am not following the rules.

Color Coded Behavior Cards

The function of the color coded behavior cards is to have the students begin their day with a set of cards placed one behind the other in the order of green, yellow, pink, and orange displayed in a pocket chart. Each time a student misbehaves they must move their first, or green, behavior card behind the rest, which will reveal the next color card of yellow and so on. Each time a student moves a color card they have a consequence. To create the color coded behavior card chart do the following:

- Place a large pocket chart at the front of the room.
- Purchase color index cards.
- Write each student's name on each card within a set containing one green, yellow, pink, and orange card.
- Make a small sign to hang above the behavior cards that explains the color coded meaning of each card and its consequence.

**Behavior Card
Color Code Key**

Green Card = Great Day

Yellow Card = First Violation/Warning

Pink Card = Second Violation/Time-Out

Orange Card = Third Violation/Note or Phone Call Home

Individual Student Behavior Modification Charts

Each academic year you will encounter, if you're lucky, a few students with behavior issues in your class. These students will respond to the class behavior chart that you implement but they will steer off the beaten path more frequently than the other students. To deal with students who are frequent offenders, consider utilizing a behavior modification chart.

Mini Behavior Charts

For each student who needs to modify his or her behavior, place a behavior mini chart on the top corner of their desk. This chart is great for focusing on one behavior that you wish to modify. Consider the following mini behavior chart uses and implement it according to your student's needs:

Problem: The student is not able to complete his or her work on time.

Solution: For each subject that the student is able to finish work on time for, they earn a sticker to place within a block on their mini behavior chart. Once they have earned ten stickers they receive a reward.

Problem: The student is not behaving during lunch.

Solution: For each day the student behaves in lunch, they earn a sticker for their chart. Once the student earns ten stickers and they have proven that they can behave during lunch for two consecutive weeks, then they can earn the right not to be on the behavior chart anymore.

Problem: The student is not able to pay attention during given directions.

Solution: For each time they are able to repeat the given directions correctly, they earn a sticker. After they have fulfilled the required sticker amount for the mini behavior chart, they can earn a reward and if necessary begin a new chart.

How to make a mini behavior chart:

- The mini chart should consist of blocks that the student must fill with stickers or smiley faces by demonstrating the appropriate behaviors necessary. The amount of blocks that need to be filled will depend on the student's needs.

- If the student earns a sticker in all of the required blocks for the day or week then they can earn a special privilege or rewards based on the student's interests.

Figure 7.3
Mini Behavior Chart Example

Formal Behavior Charts

If the student needs to modify one or two behaviors, to say the least, because he or she is becoming a disruption to the class or themselves, then implement a formal behavior chart. Formal behavior charts are completed each day by way of teacher observation and monitored with parent involvement. How to create a formal behavior chart:

- Create an age-appropriate behavior chart (see examples given in figures 7.4).
- Conduct a teacher-student conference to discuss the reasons for the behavior chart, how the formal behavior chart will be implemented, and the student's behavior goals.
- Monitor the student's desired behavior with the formal behavior chart and for each day that the student is unsuccessful with demonstrating this behavior, write detailed comments explaining why and when the student was unsuccessful.

Examples of Incomplete Comments about Behaviors	Examples of Complete Comments about Behaviors
• _____was not paying attention today.	• _____ chose not to pay attention during math instruction and therefore he didn't complete his assignment. The incomplete assignment has been placed in his folder to be completed for homework.
• _____ was talking during class.	• Instead of completing her center work, _____ chose to talk to others which became a distraction to herself and the students around her. _____ received two verbal warnings and was not allowed to participate in center activities after the third warning.
• _____ hit someone today.	• During math instruction _____ hit another student on the arm with a closed fist because they accidentally stepped on his foot. _____ received a five minute time out and apologized for this action.
• _____ did not do her work today.	• _____ was fidgeting in her pencil box and crawling under her desk during math. _____ ignored my request of getting started on her work and had to sit next to me in order to complete her assignment in a timely manner.
• _____ was not being respectful today.	• _____ was using profanity during recess. I spoke with _____ about choosing appropriate words and she assured me that it wouldn't continue.

Figure 7.4a
Early Childhood Behavior Chart

Date:

_____'s Behavior Chart

I am working on _____.
I can color the smiley face if I had a great day.

Monday	Tuesday	Wednesday

_____	_____	_____
Parent Signature	Parent Signature	Parent Signature

Thursday	Friday

_____	_____
Parent Signature	Parent Signature

Figure 7.4b
Primary Behavior Chart

Date:		
_____'s Behavior Chart		
☺ = Great ✔ = Okay X = Needs Improvement		
Goals:		
Monday		
Tuesday		
Wednesday		
Thursday		
Friday		
Parent signature required each day.		

Figure 7.4c
Intermediate Behavior Chart

Date: _____

Student: _____

Behavior Modification Chart

Behavior Scoring Rubric:

3: Super Day   2: Good Day   1: Needs Improvement   0: Unacceptable

Goals:		
Monday		
Tuesday		
Wednesday		
Thursday		
Friday		

Parent signature required for each day.

Figure 7.4d
Chunk Chart

Date: _____

Student: _____

Chunk Chart
Chunking my day for success!

☺ = Great Job   ☹ = Needs Improvement

Parent signature required for each day.

Goals:	I will have a great morning.	I will have a great afternoon.
Monday		
Tuesday		
Wednesday		
Thursday		
Friday		

Informing Parents of Student Behavior Issues

Informing the parent of the formal behavior chart which will be sent home each night is very important and must be approached delicately. It is best to call the parents or conduct a teacher-parent conference to discuss the behavior issues that are taking place. During the conference it is imperative for the parents to understand how the behavior modification chart will work and the role they will play in its implementation (signing the chart daily, communicating concerns with the teacher and their child, and reinforcing expectations).

Figure 7.5
Parent Letter for Behavior Modification Chart

Date

To the guardians of (student name),

As per our recent conversations regarding (student name) behavior choices, I am writing to inform you of a behavior modification chart that may help deter him from (state behavior issue).

I conducted a teacher-student conference with (student name) and we determined the behavior goal that he will work toward which is incorporated in the attached behavior modification chart.

Support from home will be important for the chart to have any effect on modifying the behavior. Please sign the behavior chart daily, communicate any concerns with me and your child, and help reinforce the expectations. The partnership we form should help to diminish the behavior issue at hand.
Thank you for your support.

Sincerely,

(Teacher's Name)

Time-Out

Time-out is the most widely used and appropriate form of discipline that is found in school classrooms. If you ever overhear a teacher complaining that time-out doesn't work and it's a waste of time, then they are probably not issuing it properly. The following tips should help maximize the use of time-out in your classroom:

- A time-out area should be established for the classroom and the playground. The area should be within close proximity of the teacher.
- Make sure that the punishment fits the crime. Do not take away a child's entire recess. Remember that if they don't get to run around and exert their energy they will save all that energy for when they reenter your classroom and they will most likely be disruptive throughout the rest of the day.
- During time-out the student must remain silent and not be allowed to interact with others.
- The student should be expected to do one of the following:
  — Complete the work that they chose not to do.

  — Write an apology letter or a paragraph about why they are in time-out and how they plan to solve their problem next time the issue arises. If the time-out must take place during recess then provide a clipboard and pencil for the student to take outside in order to complete their assignment.

- Before the student is allowed to rejoin the group, they must meet very briefly with the teacher to discuss their actions, consequences, and how they will solve their problem next time.

How to Manage the Line

The way students behave while walking in line to get from here to there is a direct reflection of the teacher's behavior management skills. The following techniques can be implemented to help maintain a safe and quiet line as you transport your students through the school hallways:

- Establish the *finger on lip, hand on hip* routine for the primary students. Students should place their index finger from their right hand over their lips in the *shh...* position and they should place their left hand in a fist position on their hip. By positioning their hands in this way, the student is reminded to stay quiet and keep their hands to themselves while walking in the hall.
- For the intermediate grades, let one student be your eyes by giving them a clipboard, paper, and a pen in order to walk beside the class line and write down the names of talkers and students who are not keeping their hands to themselves as they walk in line.
- All teachers should float between the front and end of the line in order to monitor the behavior of the entire class.

- For large classes or if your class is continually disruptive in the hall, the teacher may want to consider two short lines. To establish two short lines, assign students to either line A or B; another possibility is to have a boy line and a girl line. This is great for holding competitions to find the quietest line.

- Use the good choice method to provide positive reinforcement. By simply stating, "I like how Tyrell is walking in line," other students will now use Tyrell as an example and stop skipping or running in hopes of getting the same positive reinforcement.

- Provide rewards for random students who are demonstrating how to walk properly in line. For instance, randomly choose one or more students to receive a sticker or pencil and tell the students that they never know when they will be caught making a good choice in line so they must always do their best. Another reward could be to let a good role model be the line leader next time you leave the classroom or let the student who has been caught doing a great job carry something of significance while in line.

- If the students are demonstrating difficulty walking in line, then stop and wait for them to get quiet. Tell them that the time they waste in the hall will be time wasted off their recess. Float up and down the line giving them the *look of disappointment* until they are ready.

- Practice makes perfect. No matter what the student's age they will get the message that you want a quiet line even if they have to practice until perfection (especially if it's during their recess). **★Tip:** The students who consistently demonstrate good behavior while in line should not be required to practice; instead let them play while the insubordinates practice for perfection.

Praising Positive Behaviors

Rewards will be your most powerful behavior modification tool. To keep students interested in maintaining the rules and expectations you will need to reward students for following the rules. Positive reinforcement can be done on a group or individual basis. When students are caught following the rules they should be rewarded. Depending on your class dynamics, you may need to keep students motivated by changing the positive reinforcement strategy each quarter. Most importantly, never take away a reward that has been earned. For instance, don't take a marble out of the class *Good Job Jar* or take class money away from a child after he or she has earned it, even if their later actions are less than acceptable. If students are caught following the rules, use these positive reinforcement ideas to motivate them to continue being productive and safe:

- Reward students with tickets that are redeemable for special privileges such as a homework pass, gum chewing for a class period, or allowing students to drink from water bottles for a day.

- Students can earn the chance of getting their name added to a jar for a prize drawing at the end of the week. If immediate feedback is necessary for your group of students, then conduct a prize drawing at the end of each day. The prize could be something as simple as being able to take home the class pet (which is a stuffed animal) in primary grades or earn a homework pass or pencil for intermediate grades.

- Establish a good behavior currency system with class money designed by the teacher or recycled from an old board game. Students can use the money they earn to purchase items from the teacher's class store. It would be a good idea to laminate the class money so that it is reusable year after year. Letting students keep small wallets in their desks is a great way for students to store their class money.

- A class effort for good behavior could be earned by adding pom-poms, a small cup of popcorn seeds, or marbles to a *Good Job Jar*. When the jar is full, the entire class will earn a special treat or extra recess. ★**Tip:** Make sure the jar isn't so big that students lose interest in trying to fill it.

- If teamwork is needed to motivate the students, then divide the class into teams. The first group to earn twenty large paper clips or plastic links will earn a reward. Hang the paper clips or links at the front of the room to give the students a visual reminder to behave. This positive reinforcement can also be done as a whole class effort.

- Establish a *Good Choice* wall. The *Good Choice* wall gives all students the opportunity to randomly earn stickers for their mini behavior chart through good behavior. Display all of the student's mini behavior charts on a wall or on the inside of the classroom door. Once the student has earned all ten of the required stickers, they are able to choose from the prize box or earn a homework pass and receive a new mini behavior chart to be able to earn more good choice stickers. Explain to the students that they never know who or when someone will be caught making a *good choice*, so the secret is to always make good choices. The following are examples of how the *Good Choice* wall will help solve behavior issues in your classroom.

Problem: Many students are calling out the answer to the questions being asked and the teacher is becoming irritated.

Solution: Teacher says, "I like how Anil is choosing to raise his hand before he speaks. Anil, you may get a good choice sticker." As Anil walks to his good choice chart, all the other students remember to raise their hands.

Problem: Many students are not walking in a straight and quiet line in the hallway.

Solution: Teacher says, "I like how Keisha is making a good choice in line. She may get a good choice sticker when we get back to class. Let's see who else is making a good choice." As Keisha smiles, the other students scramble to become the next quietest in line.

Problem: In general your class has been very disrespectful to one another.

Solution: Teacher says, "I just overheard Marcus giving Dominic a compliment. Marcus, I am very proud, you may get a good choice sticker." As they continue to work, you hear students complimenting one another's work.

Follow these steps to create a *good choice* display:

1. Display individual *good choice* charts for each student. The *good choice* chart can be kept on the corner of each student's desk or in a class display on the wall or door. The chart should look like the mini behavior chart pictured earlier in figure 7.3.

2. If you chose to post the good choice charts on the door or wall, then place a title above the charts that reads: *We Can Make Good Choices.*

3. Place stickers in an accessible area where students can reach them in order to be able to independently place their stickers on their *good choice* chart when told to do so by the teacher.

4. Have a prize box or reward system ready for students who fill their *good choice* chart with the required amount of stickers.

Avoiding Teacher-Student Power Struggles

For any behavior management strategy to work, it is essential for the teacher to react in a fair, immediate, and consistent manner with all students in the classroom. Never engage in a battle of the wits with students. When students are able to engage you in a power struggle or cause you to become visibly frustrated, in their minds they have won, since they now have the attention of the teacher and the entire class on them. Ways to avoid a teacher–student power struggle:

- Ignore confrontational students by simply saying, "end of discussion" and continuing to teach no matter how much of a fit they throw. If the situation escalates, call or send a messenger to the office to have that student removed from your classroom. Never physically remove a student from your classroom since that is what your guidance counselor and principal are there for.

- If a student wants an explanation of what they did wrong, as if they didn't already know, tell them that you will discuss the issue with them after class, at recess, or before dismissal.

- If you are engaged in a group activity and a student becomes disruptive and jeopardizes the group's safety, ask the student to go back to their seat. If the disruptive students refuse to leave the group, then move the group away from the disruptive student.

- For students with anger management issues, create a small area in the class where they can escape to and calm themselves down. In this designated area you might have a carpet square for them to sit on, a stress ball to squeeze, a puzzle to distract their anger, and paper and pen for them to vent their frustrations.

- If a student clearly does not want to be in your classroom and is refusing to join group activities, then just leave them be. This type of behavior is mostly evident in primary grades. Don't mistake this behavior as trying to be disrespectful because sometimes it's simply separation anxiety, shyness, or the child has yet to develop coping skills. Be sure to keep a close eye on this student, but give them time to warm up before becoming part of the group. If possible, provide activities that are fun in order to lure them back into the group. When they decide to join the group, do not make a big deal about it, just go on teaching as normal so not to embarrass or frighten the student away.

- Give the student a choice to make. The following are examples of how to give students choices in order to modify their behavior:

  Problem: A student is refusing to complete their work.

  Choices: The teacher says, "Okay, you have a choice, finish your work now or finish your work during recess."

  Problem: A student refuses to demonstrate their best work.

  Choices: The teacher says, "You have a choice, finish your work neatly now or you can redo the activity for homework."

  Problem: A student continues to disrupt the class.

  Choices: The teacher says, "You have a choice, behave and complete your work in the classroom or complete your work in the office."

  ★**Tip:** Most importantly, never yell. To let the student know that you mean business, speak in a low, deep, and authoritative voice.

Deterring Behavior Issues Using Good Instruction

Good instruction can lend a helping hand to help deter behavior issues. Good instruction does not just include delivering a good lesson, it should also incorporate motivating transitions, limited down time, speaking and lecturing less, and allowing for wiggles and movement.

Transitions

Between teaching subjects and activities during each lesson, the teacher must provide interesting transitions that will motivate students as they move from one activity to the next. Here are a few motivating transition ideas:

- Begin the lesson with an attention grabber such as a story, a real-world object, or an interesting question related to the learning.
- Use listening games to move students to and from areas around the room. For instance, say to the students, "If you are wearing a blue shirt you may join me at the carpet area. If you are wearing a red shirt you may have a seat on the carpet," and so on.
- Give the students five seconds each to use the water fountain when taking a group break. The person directly behind the student at the water fountain will count so they know when their time is up.
- Provide time limits by counting slowly to five as students transition from one area to another or as they put away their things to get ready for the next activity, otherwise valuable teaching time can be wasted.

- Move students from one area to another by allowing boys to go first, then girls, and tell them that they are in a competition to see which group is the quietest as they go to the designated area.

- Tell students that you expect them to walk *quiet like mice* from one designated area to the next.

- Include movement throughout the lesson, such as cooperative group activities, role playing, creating work stations with manipulatives, or moving the group to different areas of the room to perform different tasks.

- Transition the students by allowing them to practice their learning in unconventional ways, such as using mini chalkboards or wipe boards as they work in groups using the floor as a work area.

Regaining Attention

Losing the group's attention during a lesson can be frustrating. At first it starts as a small disruption involving two or three students, and if ignored more students may become disruptive, and before you know it you will have a wildfire of inattentive students to deal with. So, put out those disruptive fires as soon as they start with these helpful tips:

- Establish a class clap (a clap pattern) that students must complete in order to show they are ready to listen and learn. For example:

  Clap-Clap   *Clap-Clap-Clap*
  slow– slow   fast– fast– fast

- Say in a low voice, "If you can hear me, clap once, if you can hear me clap twice, if you can hear me clap three times." Continue until you have everyone's attention.

- Say in a low voice, "If you can hear me, put your hands on your head. If you can hear me, put your hands on your shoulders. If you can hear me, put your hands on your knees." Continue until you have everyone's attention.

- Use the statement, "One, two, three, eyes on me." Repeat until everyone is ready, and if need be use close proximity when making the statement by standing next to the disruptive student or students.

- Turn off the lights or shake a maraca or tambourine for a moment to regain student attention.

Limiting Down Time

Limiting down time simply means not to waste any teaching or learning time. You can monitor the amount of down time in your room by incorporating these ideas:

- Give time limits on activities by using the classroom clock, a digital timer, or a cooking timer. Give students a five-minute and one-minute warning to complete finishing touches on assignments before their time is up.

- If your students are too young to be able to tell time, then explain time limits by using the minute hand on the classroom clock. For example, when the big hand gets on the five, our time is up.

- Have your lesson plans and supplies ready and nearby so that no time is wasted searching for materials (subject bins are very efficient, see ch.3 for more information).

- Give students who finish their work early a bonus question, or allow them to challenge themselves by creating their own question or problem on the back of their assignment. Early finishers could also be in charge of clean up or collecting materials.

- If you have finished teaching your lesson but still have five or ten minutes left before the next lesson activity is scheduled to begin, then consider reading a book to the students from the class library or have the students clean and organize their work space.

Teaching without Lecturing

Too much speaking and lecturing can make a student lose interest in what you are trying to teach. Be aware of when you have lost your student's interest and be able to shift gears to regain their attention. Take the following into consideration when teaching:

- Don't speak at the students but instead, include the students in a class discussion.

- Do not reiterate rules or facts over and over. If your students heard you the first time, that's all they need.

- Do not let individual students monopolize the floor when it comes to speaking. Give everyone a fair chance to share by monitoring student share time.

- Read your student's body language; if they appear to be fidgeting or talkative then chances are they have lost interest.

- Keep the students involved and focused. Ask students to repeat what was just said either by you or by a fellow student. Call on students randomly using talking sticks (keep a class set of popsicle sticks in a bucket that bear student names and if the teacher pulls a student's popsicle stick from the bucket, then that is the student expected to respond).

- Make it interesting—if you are excited about the learning then the students will be too. When you are speaking to the class, move about the room, incorporate visuals, use voice inflection, and hand movements.

Allowing for Wiggles and Movement

Who said students have to be sitting in a chair in order to learn? A school day can be very long, especially from the elementary student's point of view. Break up the monotony by giving the gift of movement. Movement will help circulate more oxygen to the students' brains and they will therefore be more apt to learn. Here are some simple suggestions for providing wiggles and movement throughout the day:

- Give wiggle workouts between subjects or, now don't be afraid, sometimes in the middle of a lesson. If student behavior is becoming an issue or if they look tired, stop what you're doing and tell them to stand up for a wiggle workout. A wiggle workout is a quick one or two minute, teacher led, series of exercises that provides students with an intermission. When the workout is over, students are expected to regain their composure and focus on their learning.

- Provide opportunities for students to complete their assignment on the floor or let them use their chair seat as a desk while they sit on the floor. Giving this freedom of movement every now and then will help motivate student learning.

- Give the students the freedom to choose where they would like to sit during a lesson.

- Get a breath of fresh air by reading to the students outside or by letting the students complete an assignment outside under a tree.

- Let students work with partners or share their completed work with other classes.

How to Deal with the Student Who...

Throughout the year you may find yourself saying, "As if planning and implementing a lesson weren't enough work, the students are trying to drive me crazy by acting up in class and, of all days, during my observation." As frustrating as this may be, the truth is, before learning can occur the classroom must be orderly and students must feel safe in their learning environment. The following behavior management strategies should help you cope with specific behavior problems.

Can't Sit Still...

- Give the student jobs such as passing out papers, distributing or collecting materials, erasing the chalkboard, organizing the classroom library, peer teacher, class messenger, watering the plants, and computer time.

- Incorporate movement in your lessons as much as possible.

Calls Out...

- Do not reward the student who calls out by listening to what they have to say.
- Tell the student that you would love to hear what they would like to share but you can't because they didn't raise their hand to speak.
- Call on a student who raised their hand and praise them for it by saying, "Christina, I like how you raised your hand to speak, so you may share what you are thinking."

Fidgets...

- Turn the student's desk around so that the opening or storage area of their desk is facing away from them.
- Do not allow pencil sharpeners or mechanical lead pencils to be used in your classroom.
- Limit the amount of crayons and supplies that a student may keep in their desk at any given time.

Doesn't Complete the Work on Time...

- Set a timer to limit how long the student has to complete their task.
- Give positive praise and reward the student for completing their work on time (see mini behavior chart shown in figure 7.3).
- Give the student a choice: either complete the work during the assigned time or complete the work at recess.
- Provide close proximity between teacher and student.

Has Focusing Issues...

- Ask the student to repeat directions or recall what was just said.
- Give the student a pair of headphones (remove the cord) to wear in order to block out distracting sounds around them.
- Let the student work in a carrel to block out distractions around the room. If a carrel is not available then create one for a desktop by taping three pieces of cardboard together to form a makeshift carrel.

Spends Too Much Time in the Bathroom...

- Place a clipboard with a bathroom sign-out sheet clipped to it by the classroom door.
- Put a digital wristwatch on the clipboard above the sign-out sheet for students to write their names and the times they leave and come back from the bathroom.
- If the student goes to the bathroom too frequently and for a few days in a row, then speak to the parents about any issues the child may be experiencing.

Refuses to Join the Group...

- Mostly occurs in the beginning of the year or when the student has a particularly bad day.
- Do not make a big deal about the fact that the student doesn't want to join the group.
- Tell them privately that they may join the group when they feel ready.
- This type of behavior could occur for as long as a week. Just be sure to keep an eye on their activity and before long they will get bored and rejoin the group.
- If this behavior lasts longer than a week, then you must meet with the counselor and parents.

Doesn't Participate...

- If a child is shy they tend not to participate often. Try and find out the real reason why they refuse to participate; maybe they are upset or possibly they have a speech impediment. Seek help from the guidance counselor or the speech pathologist if this is the case.
- Use talking sticks to randomly call on students. Sometimes it goes unnoticed that some students are rarely called on. To make and utilize talking sticks, follow these directions:
  1. Buy craft sticks, enough for each student.
  2. Write each student's name on an individual stick.
  3. Place the talking sticks in a box (an empty tissue box works well).
  4. When selecting someone from the class to answer a question, pull a talking stick out of the box. The name on the stick that you pull will be the student required to answer the question.

Doesn't Do Their Homework...

- Offer a reward system for completing homework.
- Display a chart that documents which students have completed their homework each night.
- Have students complete homework at recess if it is not completed the night before.

Frequently Misses Their Parents...

- Allow the student to bring in a picture of their parent and keep it on their desk.
- Let the student draw a picture or write a letter to their parent.
- Keep a small stuffed animal handy for students to keep on their desk if they are sad.
- Allow the student to bring in a flannel shirt or sweater that belongs to their parent so it can be worn by the student when they begin to miss him or her.

Cries Obsessively...

- Sometimes students cry and you can sympathize with that; however, if the crying is obsessive and frequent it can get downright annoying. Tell the student that they need to stop the tears because they have a job to do.
- Ignore the frequent crier, do not pamper or give them any extra attention since this may be their purpose for crying in the first place.
- If crying continues for more than a week, then seek help from the school counselor and the student's parents.
- Reward the student for putting away their tears with positive praise, a sticker, or a happy note home.

Hits, Bites, or Throws Things...

- Any time a student hurts another student or the teacher by hitting, biting, or throwing things, they need to be immediately removed from the classroom by a school counselor or administrator. Call or send a student to the office for assistance.
- While waiting for help, try to calm the student down, and if that doesn't work move the entire class to the opposite side of the room away from the student posing a threat until assistance arrives.
- All students who have been hit or bitten must be evaluated by the nurse and their parents must be contacted. If the nurse doesn't send a note home, it becomes your responsibility to inform the parents of the incident.

Has Anger Management Issues...

- Teach anger management strategies to the student or as a group activity.
- Explain how to solve problems by role playing or conducting a group discussion.
- Teach students calming or breathing techniques such as "close your eyes and take three deep breaths."
- Give the student a stress ball to squeeze when they become angry.
- For the student with severe anger management issues, give them a special area in the room to sit and calm down in. That area should contain items of interest for the student so they can take their mind off of their feelings of anger.
- Schedule visits for the student with the school counselor and keep in contact with the parents.
- For safety reasons, never let other students in your class escort students with serious behavior problems to the office. Administration or guidance counselors must be called upon for this task.
- Keep your cell phone readily available for calling parents (or threatening to call parents).

Is Shy...

- Try not to put the shy student on the spot.
- Give the student a cue that you are going to call on them before you actually do so. For instance; if you tug once on your right ear, the shy student is forewarned that they are about to be called on and they need to start gathering their thoughts.
- Give positive praise for all answers or contributions that the student gives.

Openly Defies You...

- Never get into a teacher-student power struggle.
- Act as if the student's actions are not bothering you (even though you are probably boiling mad inside), and continue to teach.
- If the student becomes too obnoxious to ignore and a distraction for the others, then have the defiant student removed from your class by the school counselor or an administrator.

Runs Away from the Group...

- If a child runs from the class follow these steps:
  1. Never leave the whole class, unattended, instead get help either by calling the office or getting a teacher next door to you to watch both classes while you pursue the student.
  2. While you pursue the student, have another classmate or teacher go to the office to summons assistance.
  3. Keep the student in sight by following or talking the student into stopping. If the student will not walk back to the school or office with you, then wait for the school counselor or administrator to physically bring the student back. Unless you have received special training, a teacher may not restrain or physically move a student.
- If the student frequently runs away from the group, request that the school purchases walkie-talkies so that you can quickly contact the office for assistance. Request a meeting with the parents and administrators for more suggestions, consequences for the student, and support.

Can't Stay Organized...

- Provide an organization system for the student's desk, such as a large box lid that can fit inside a desk and be pulled out like a drawer to put books, journals, folders, and materials on.
- Limit the amount of supplies that the student is allowed to keep in their desk or pencil box.

Isn't Responsible Enough to Attend a Field Trip...

- Require the student's parent to attend the field trip. If the parent cannot attend, then the student cannot attend. While the rest of the class is on the field trip, the student who is unable to attend should spend the day in a class that is one grade level below or above their grade level. Be sure the teacher is willing to accommodate the student for the day.

Bullies Others...

- Conduct frequent class discussions and incorporate role playing and reading books related to feelings and ways to deal with bullies (walk away, ignore, don't let a bully know they are bothering you, tell an adult).
- Explain that bullies only bother others because they have low self-esteem and because bullies feel bad, they want others to feel bad also.
- Assign the student who has been identified as the class bully to help out in other classrooms such as pre-kindergarten or kindergarten to help that student develop compassion as they work with others.
- Select the class bully as a volunteer to help with or teach mini lessons to younger children about how to cope with bullies.
- Meet with the bully's parents in order to place the student on a behavior chart if the above suggestions do not have an effect on their behavior.
- Reward the student for acts of kindness displayed toward others.

Destroys Property...

- Expect the student to fix, clean up, or replace what has been destroyed or vandalized.
- Require the student to write an apology note to the janitor or whomever the damage directly affects.
- Explain to the students that they are part owners of everything in the class and when they destroy something in the classroom, they destroy something that belongs to everyone in the class.
- Establish a *classroom watch program* that works like a neighborhood watch program. When a student sees someone destroying property, they should immediately inform an adult.

Tattle Tales...

- At the beginning of the year, inform students that they are to only tell the teacher about emergencies such as someone getting hurt or hurting someone else. All other problems need to be resolved by using their words to tell the person who is bothering them how they feel.
- Role play with students modeling how to tell someone how they feel about something they don't like. Teach them to use the phrase, "I don't like when you _____ so please stop."
- Stop the tattle tale before they have a chance to explain their tattle by saying, "Stop, is this a tattle or an emergency? If it's not an emergency then solve your problem on your own by using your words to tell the person how you feel."

Steals from Others...

- Address the class when something is *missing*. Explain that the old saying, "Finders keepers, losers weepers" does not apply in this classroom.
- Provide a basket for lost and found items and reward students for their honesty when items are returned. ★**Tip:** If two students claim ownership to the same item then the teacher should keep the item in question in their desk and tell the students that their parents will be contacted in order to find out who the true owner of the item is. Usually one student will crack and say not to call their parents because "they just remembered" it's not theirs. Another way to find out who is the true owner of the item is to see who is more visibly upset over losing the item until their parents are contacted.

Uses Profanity...

- Speak to the student privately about using appropriate language.
- Give the student a better choice of words to use other than profanity, such as "fooey, sugar, or cheese and crackers."

Chapter 8
Home–School Connection Ideas

A relationship of trust and communication between home and school is an important part of having a successful year. A teacher-parent partnership begins when the parent is confident in knowing the following:

1. That the teacher will treat their child with kindness and respect.

2. That their child is being challenged to perform at their individual best.

3. That the teacher promptly returns phone calls, E-mails, or notes and is available (with a smile) to discuss their child's problems or academic progress.

Chapter eight will provide you with home-school connection ideas for homework, Back-to-School night, communication, parent volunteers, conferences, and American Education week.

Preparing for Back-to-School Night or Open House

Back-to-School Night or Open House can be a nerve-racking experience but with the right planning you will surely be a success. So, let's get ready! Use these steps to help you prepare:

1. Send out a reminder to parents about the Back-to-School Night the day before. Include the date, times, and a small note stating how much you look forward to meeting with them. (I know, but it sounds nice.)

2. Have the students prepare a card or self-portrait for their parents to see when they arrive at their child's desk.

3. If you haven't done so already, prepare a teacher autobiography for the parents. Include your name, the colleges you've attended, your degrees, your teaching experiences, and the excitement that you feel about being able to work with their child this year.

4. Using an outline format, create an important information sheet that explains:

   — The times that school officially begins and ends

   — The daily schedule

   — The grading policy

   — What students will be taking home each night (folders, homework, notebooks, textbooks)

   — The homework procedure

   — The procedure for birthdays (no parties during class, can bring in cupcakes to be distributed at lunch)

— The absent note requirements

— Volunteer information

— What to do if your child is to go home using a different mode of transportation than normal

— The class rules and behavior consequences

— Field trips and how field trip chaperones will be chosen (randomly with a fair chance for everyone to attend at least one trip)

— The units that will be taught for each subject throughout the year (a copy of the long range plan could be attached)

5. Make cue cards or an overhead transparency of the information being presented and use it as a guide during your presentation. You should also staple the information sheet to the teacher autobiography so the parents have a copy.

6. Display examples of the report card and the textbooks that students will be using for each subject. These items are best displayed on the reading table area for the parents to thumb through.

7. Instruct the students to straighten up the classroom and their desks at the end of the day so the room is presentable for the parents.

8. Place a desk outside of your classroom for the parent sign-in sheet (copy the parent sign-in sheet shown in figure 8.1). You may choose to spruce up the desk by placing a table cloth, a small welcome sign, and a bowl of candy on top. Don't forget to provide a couple of pens for signing in, a wish list of donations needed for the classroom, and extra student supply lists, just in case some of the parents still haven't purchased the necessary materials.

9. Allow time for parents to look around the room and inside their child's desk.

10. This night is not for conferencing about individual student progress. If a parent tries to trap you in a conference dialogue, explain to them that this isn't really a good time to conduct conferences but you would be more than happy to meet with them at a later scheduled time. To avoid this situation, you may even want to mention in your opening statement that tonight is not for conferencing.

11. Relax and be confident because you are the one with a degree in education and there is a certain respect that comes with that.

Figure 8.1
Parent Sign-in Sheet

Welcome! Please Sign In	
Parent Name:	Student Name:

Establishing Lines of Communication

Parents want to be involved and informed when it comes to their child's education. Lines of communication between home and school can be formed in many ways. Below are home-school communication examples that will make your students' parents feel as if your classroom door is always open to them.

Monthly Newsletters

- On the first of each month send home a newsletter that gives insight to the units of study and focus skills that will be taught, field trips or assemblies that will take place, important reminders, and outstanding student accomplishments.
- Give your newsletter a little flare by adding clip art and jazzy fonts.
- Put your newsletter on color paper to grab the parent's attention.
- Do not let your newsletter exceed more than one page in length. Parents are busy and they may not read it if it's any longer. See figures 8.2 and 8.3 for examples of class newsletter formats.

Figure 8.2
Example Newsletter Format

Kindergarten Newsletter
Name of the Month

Open the newsletter with a short introduction paragraph that mentions important information or reminders.

Reading:

Math: Write brief
                             statements
                             about the
                             units that
Science: that will be
                             taught during
Writing: each subject
                             for the month.

Hats off to the following students for being successful with _____.

(list student names)

Figure 8.3
Example Newsletter Format

The Kindergarten Gazette
Name of the Month

| **Teacher's Corner:** Include a short introduction paragraph that mentions important information. | **Reminders:** State any field trip dates, school closings, assemblies, due dates for projects, etc. |
| **About Academics:**

  Reading:

  Writing:

  Math:

  Science: | **Student Spotlight:** Share three to five student success stories each month. Be sure to name every student by the end of the year. |

Ways to Win Parents Over

- Call or write a note to parents letting them know about the *good* things that their child has been caught doing. Parents usually receive teacher phone calls and notes in reference to bad news and by breaking this pattern you will brighten the parent's day.
- Make one positive *just because* phone call or written note per week until all students have had a turn to receive one.
- Make time for parents and respond to their questions, notes, or phone calls the same day you receive them.

Informing Parents of Difficulties

- Sometimes the not-so-happy phone call or note is unavoidable. No matter how angry you may feel about the situation that the phone call or note is in reference to, you must maintain a pleasant disposition at all times. Remember, the parents want you to care for their child unconditionally, so don't give them reason to doubt that.
- If you are informing a parent about an incident that involved more than just their child, do not mention the names of the other children involved. You don't want the possibility of parents confronting one another and a neighborhood rift occurring.
- Be certain that the parent actually receives notes that are sent home by providing a space for a parent signature. Call the parent if the note doesn't come back signed the following day.

E-Mails

- Teachers should not give their personal phone number to students or parents, instead provide them with a professional E-mail address.
- Give parents your professional E-mail address on Back-to-School night.
- E-mails are great if a student is prone to *losing* notes or if you are having a hard time getting in touch with parents by phone. They also provide documentation of your efforts to reach the child's guardians even if they refuse to contact you back.

Utilizing Parent Volunteers

Sometimes you get lucky and the parent volunteers are irreplaceable. They come in, get right to work, and don't need much direction. And sometimes you get parent volunteers who mean well, but... you get the picture. To avoid the *but they mean well* situation, most schools offer a parent volunteer workshop that is mandatory before parents can volunteer their time in the classroom. Whether your volunteers have or have not been trained, here are a few tips for getting the most out of their much appreciated time:

- Have a volunteer basket ready and waiting for either the frequent volunteer or the *I just thought I'd show up today volunteer.* Item ideas for the volunteer basket:
  — A written request for all volunteers to turn off their cell phones.

  — Written directions for working with students, a list of students to work with, and the necessary manipulatives (flash cards, books, activities, stickers, etc).

  — Written directions for making flashcards, sorting manipulatives for activities, creating center items, designing bulletin boards, copying work sheets, and all the materials necessary to do so.

- Maintain an area within the room or a common area outside of the classroom for volunteers to have a place to work.

- For parents who would like to volunteer but don't have the time during the day, send home a volunteer bag with directions for making, cutting, coloring, or sorting materials.

Homework

I lost it, I left it at school yesterday, my baby sister ripped it up, I had a game last night… and the all-time classic, my dog ate it. This is just a small list of excuses that you will hear when it comes time to collect homework assignments. To avoid as many excuses as possible you must be very clear with the students and parents about the homework expectations and routine. It is also important for the teacher to establish a manageable routine for assigning and grading homework so that this little side note of teaching doesn't become the reason for a developing ulcer.

Assigning Homework

Like everything else in the field of teaching, there is no one way to establish a homework routine. Consider your students' age and abilities when designing your homework criteria. Here are a few homework ideas to help you get started:

- Students could maintain a labeled homework pocket folder that will contain the homework assignments that the teacher distributes each afternoon.

- Students could keep a labeled homework journal in which the homework assignment or activity sheet is glued horizontally to the first available page in the journal each afternoon.

- Students could maintain a labeled spiral homework notebook in which the homework assignment is copied from the board and dated by the student. Copying homework assignments from the board is best done as part of the student's morning work activities before announcements.

- Students could receive a monthly homework calendar that specifies each day's homework assignment. This homework activity is best for primary grades and should contain one or two tasks per day that reflect the units of study for the month. See example shown in figure 8.4.

- Students could work from a homework sheet that gives repetitive tasks for each day of the week, which should be referenced and kept on their refrigerator for the entire quarter. Each quarter a new homework sheet should be sent home with new steps to follow. See example shown in figure 8.5.

- Students could receive differentiated homework by filling in the blanks on a generic weekly homework sheet (can be filled in by teacher or students). See example shown in figure 8.6.

Figure 8.4
Partial Example of Homework Calendar

May Homework Calendar				
1. Complete the assigned activity each day. 2. Ask an adult to write their initials on the calendar day after the activity is completed. 3. Return your calendar to your teacher at the end of the month.				
Monday	**Tuesday**	**Wednesday**	**Thursday**	**Friday**
Write your full name ten times.	Draw a self portrait and write 3 words that describe you.	Practice writing the alphabet using capital letters.	Practice writing the alphabet using lower case letters.	Sort the coins from a handful of change.
Count 100 pennies.	Explain and practice 3 good manners while eating dinner.	Read a story to someone older than you.	Tell an adult about the classroom rules that you must follow.	Write a sentence by sounding out the words. Draw a picture to match the sentence.

Figure 8.5
Quarterly Homework Sheet Example

Second Quarter Homework Sheet

Monday:
    Step #1: Read a story from your anthology to an adult.
    Step #2: Complete the math worksheet that was sent home.
    Step #3: Practice writing your spelling words five times each.

Tuesday:
    Step #1: Read a story from your anthology to an adult.
             Draw a picture about your favorite part of the story.
    Step #2: Complete the math worksheet that was sent home.
    Step #3: Write sentences using your spelling words.

Wednesday:
    Step #1: Read a story from your anthology to an adult.
             Identify the main idea of the story by writing and drawing.
    Step #2: Complete the math worksheet that was sent home.
    Step #3: Illustrate your spelling words.

Thursday:
    Step #1: Read a story from your anthology to an adult.
             Write five words that you learned from this story.
    Step #2: Complete the math worksheet that was sent home.
    Step #3: Practice for your spelling test.

Figure 8.6
Blank Homework Sheet

Homework Sheet

Week of: **Group:**

Monday:
    1. Reading _____
    2. Math _____
    3. Spelling _____

Tuesday:
    1. Reading _____
    2. Math _____
    3. Spelling _____

Wednesday:
    1. Reading _____
    2. Math _____
    3. Spelling _____

Thursday:
    1. Reading _____
    2. Math _____
    3. Spelling _____

Collecting and Grading Homework

- Homework could be collected and graded on a daily, weekly, or monthly basis depending on the expectations and type of assignments.
- Homework doesn't necessarily need to be collected. Students can place their homework on the corner of their desk. As they complete their morning work, the teacher or a homework helper can walk from desk to desk and stamp the completed homework. All incomplete homework should be put in a designated basket and completed at recess.
- In order to monitor who has or has not completed their homework, you can display a homework chart. Each time the student completes their homework they can add a sticker to the homework chart. One quick glance at the chart will let you know who is and is not completing their homework.

Communicating Homework Expectations with Students

Take the time to meet with your students by conducting a whole group discussion about the homework policy that you wish to implement in your classroom. Students need to understand the homework expectations before homework is distributed for completion. Follow these tips to help prepare your class for their homework responsibilities:

- Students should understand that homework is their responsibility and not their parent's responsibility.
- Students should understand that all incomplete homework will be completed during their recess the following day.
- Explain to the students that completing homework is part of their job since it counts toward their participation grade.
- Make it understood that their parents will also be made fully aware of the homework expectations.

Communicating Homework Expectations with Parents

- Send a homework information letter to the parents. Explain in detail the homework routine, expectations, grading, and consequences for incomplete homework. Provide a detachable portion on the letter for the parents and students to sign and return that states they have read and fully understand the homework policy. See the parent homework letter example shown in figure 8.7.

Figure 8.7
Parent Homework Letter Example

Homework Information

Date

Dear Parents,

We will begin homework assignments tomorrow night. Our class has discussed the following:

1. Homework will be assigned Monday through Thursday unless otherwise notified.
2. Homework can be found in the student's blue pocket folder labeled *Homework*.
3. Homework should be completed each night and returned the following day.
4. Homework is the student's responsibility, not the parent's responsibility.
5. Incomplete homework will be completed during recess.
6. Homework assignments will count as 50% of the student's participation grade.

Please review these items with your child and discuss the importance of completing homework consistently, setting a homework time, and remembering to bring the homework in to school each day.

- -

Detach, sign, and send back to school.

We have read, discussed, and understand the homework expectations for _____ grade.

_____   _____
Parent Signature   Student Signature

Report Card Comments

Teachers must be quite crafty when it comes to wording report card comments. This process can take weeks and hours of your time unless you have a list of report card comment ideas to help get you started. Here are a few report card comment examples to help get you through this busy time of year:

Opening Remarks

Always begin the comments with a positive remark. There is good in every child even if the student has been a thorn in your side since day one of school; a positive statement must be made in order to soften the blow when giving the not-so-positive statements.

- _____ is an active student who consistently participates in class activities.
- _____ has been an excellent student role model within our class.
- _____ has had praiseworthy attendance this quarter.
- _____ is a productive student who demonstrates his best efforts when completing assignments.
- _____ is a dependable student who goes out of his way to be helpful in the classroom.
- _____ is a sociable student who has acquired many friends this year.
- I am very impressed with _____ knowledge of technology. _____ enjoys working on computer-oriented activities and troubleshooting in order to correct computer problems.
- _____ proves to be investing her greatest efforts as she continues to do her personal best in class.
- _____ is very positive toward setting learning goals and works very hard in class to meet her goal expectations.
- I am pleased with the academic advancement _____ has made in (_subject_).

Behavior Comments

Behavior comments can be addressed after a positive comment has been made. Do not overwhelm the parent with many behavior issues to work on with their child; instead focus on one or two main issues that you would like resolved, and then once those are under control focus on the next most important issue, and so forth. If the behavior is a serious issue then you should also request a conference with the parent to discuss the implementation of a behavior modification chart that will monitor the student during class in order to help resolve the behavior issue (see ch.7 for behavior chart examples).

- I would like to see _____ practice self-control over (_name behavior issue_).

- I would like _____ to improve his coping skills by being able to solve more of his problems independently and with less emotion.

- _____ is working on raising his hand and waiting his turn to speak.

- _____ is working toward being respectful to others by keeping her hands and feet to herself.

- _____'s goal is to listen more attentively when being given directions and to focus more on completing her assignments.

- _____'s main goal is to stay focused and complete the activity at hand without distracting herself or others around her.

Reading
Above Average Comments

- I am very pleased with the above average advancements _____ has made with his reading progress.

- _____ is doing an outstanding job in reading and is currently reading above grade level expectations.

- _____ uses a variety of reading strategies to decode unfamiliar words. He immediately identifies the part of the word he knows and then blends the sounds together to read the word.

- _____ is very focused and enjoys participating during reading group activities.

- _____ is consistently using the reading strategies she has learned to decode unfamiliar words.

- _____ is demonstrating fluency and is able to comprehend what has been read.

- _____ is demonstrating outstanding reading skills such as comprehension, fluency, and voice inflection.

- I can always count on _____ to share interesting facts and insights connected to the text we are reading.

- Keep up the great work in reading!

Reading
Average Comments

- I am satisfied with _____'s reading progress. He is currently reading on grade level.

- _____ is doing her very best in reading and is currently reading within grade level expectations.

- _____ frequently uses the reading strategies he has learned to decode unfamiliar words.

- To help build on _____'s progress and ability in reading, please read with him each night for at least fifteen minutes.

- _____'s reading goal is to become a more fluent reader and to do so she must practice reading at a faster pace.

- _____ is focused and seems to enjoy participating during reading group.

- _____ is demonstrating improvement in reading skills such as comprehension, fluency, and voice inflection.

- _____ is demonstrating improvement with his reading fluency and ability to comprehend what has been read.

- To help build on _____'s comprehension skills, please encourage him to read a story and reflect on what he has read by recalling characters, setting, story events, and details.

- Reviewing the sight words with _____ each night would be a great benefit to her reading ability. She is a good reader, however with more practice she has the potential to be an even better reader.

Reading
Below Average Comments

When informing a parent about their child reading below the expected reading level, it is imperative that you also provide information on the extra services that he or she is receiving in order to help close the learning gap. Many parents will also want written suggestions on what they can do to help their child become a better reader.

- _____ is trying and giving his very best in reading but is currently reading below grade level.

- _____ is currently reading just below the expected reading level at this point in the year.

- _____ is receiving independent and teacher guided practice with sight words and reading on a daily basis.

- _____ will continue to receive independent and teacher guided reading practice through a reading intervention on a daily basis. During this reading intervention he will focus on identifying sight words and using reading strategies to decode words.

- Continue to read with _____ each night for fifteen minutes. Each time _____ reads to you build on her comprehension skills by asking questions such as: What was the story about? Who were the main characters? What was the setting of the story? What was the problem and the solution? Explain why you did or did not like the story.

- _____ seems to really show an interest in the topic of transportation. Books from the library on cars, trucks, and airplanes may help spark his excitement for reading at home.

- _____ is working on using the reading strategies in order to help him to decode unfamiliar text. I have attached a copy of the reading strategies that we use in class. Please refer to these strategies when helping him practice reading at home.

- Although _____'s reading level reflects below average, she has made great strides in reading. She is now able to track or point to the words as she reads, she is beginning to use reading strategies to decode words, she has increased her sight vocabulary, and she is using the picture clues to help better understand the text.

- _____ is working on improving his fluency or pacing during reading. Improving his fluency will help him to comprehend the story events.

- _____ is developing his sight vocabulary which should help him improve his fluency and comprehension during reading.

- _____ is working on improving her ability to comprehend what she has read.

- At home there are many fun ways to help _____ with making progress in reading. Each night let her choose a bedtime story that she can either listen to or read to you. You could also play word games to help her recognize words on sight. Game ideas are: Memory, Scrabble, Go Fish (with words), and pocket words (3 words on index cards that she can carry around with her in her pocket and pull out any time to practice).

Math
Above Average Comments

- _____ is doing an excellent job in math class and is currently performing above the average expectations.

- _____ works well with the manipulatives and in cooperative groups and is currently performing above average expectations.

- _____ is doing very well in math. He has been selected as a peer tutor to help fellow students who are struggling.

- _____'s ability to clearly explain the procedure and strategies that he has used to solve algorithms is outstanding.

- _____ is doing so well in math that she is now being challenged with questions related to our math unit that require a higher level of thinking and reasoning.

Math
Average Comments

- I am proud of _____'s consistent progress in math class which has enabled him to perform at the expected grade level expectations.

- _____ is doing a great job in math class and is currently performing at expected grade level expectations.

- _____'s goal is to use proper formation and direction when writing numerals.

- _____ handles the math manipulatives and participates in cooperative group activities very well.

- _____ has demonstrated the ability to complete his math assignments accurately and on time.

- _____ has shown great improvement in his arithmetic capabilities. Keep up the good work!

Math
Below Average Comments

- _____ is currently working with a peer tutor to help improve his math skills.

- _____ is learning to communicate and participate more during cooperative group activities.

- Encourage _____ to practice the basic addition and subtraction facts to 10 as often as possible.

- Continue to review the multiplication facts with _____ as often as possible.

- _____ seems to frustrate easily when trying to complete math activities. She has set a goal for herself that requires management of these frustrations.

- _____ is performing below average in math due to his lack of focus during instruction. We will begin the implementation of the behavior chart that was discussed on (*insert date*) in order to monitor this issue.

- _____ has not been consistent with completing his math class work or homework activities.

Writing
Early Primary Comments

- In writing _____ is expressing himself on paper through descriptive pictures and beginning sounds of words. The goal _____ is working toward is *stretch spelling.* Stretch spelling is the ability to say the word slowly in order to hear and be able to write all of the sounds within that word.

- _____ is expressing her ideas and thoughts on paper through inventive spelling. Inventive spelling is one of the beginning stages in writing which the student *stretch spells* or writes the sounds they hear within words. Along with inventive spelling, students are using their resources such as the teacher, reading materials, the dictionary, and the classroom word wall to demonstrate *book spelling* or correct spellings.

- _____ has shown much improvement with the formation of letters and placing appropriate space between words.

Writing
Above Average Comments

- _____ is consistently applying capitalization, proper usage of words, punctuation, and correct spelling during writing assignments.

- _____ is demonstrating excellent writing skills by consistently remembering to include the main idea or topic sentence, details that support the main idea, attention to the audience, and a concluding sentence.

- _____ is doing a wonderful job with expressing his ideas in complete thoughts and logically organizing information when writing.

Writing
Average Comments

- _____ is trying to improve her writing skills by being more consistent with applying capitalization and punctuation marks.

- _____ needs to work on using resources such as the class word wall, a dictionary, or reading materials in order to help her spell words correctly.

- _____ has set a goal for writing with neat penmanship.

Writing
Below Average Comments

- There are many fun ways to encourage _____ with making progress in writing. Writing ideas are writing letters to family members, helping an adult write a grocery list, or keeping a journal or diary.

- _____ has set a goal for trying to write more legibly.

- _____ has set a goal for expressing her ideas in complete thoughts and logically organizing information as she writes.

End of the Year Comments

- _____ has worked very hard and has made great strides this year.

- I am very impressed with _____'s academic achievements this year.

- Continue to provide _____ with encouragement and support as she works her way through the third grade curriculum next year.

- I can't stress enough how important it is to your child's success to continue to read throughout the summer and as often as possible. The public library has wonderful reading programs available for students to participate in while on summer vacation.

- As mentioned during our conference last month, I would encourage summer school as a consideration for _____. Summer school would benefit his academic progress for the next school year. You will find the necessary information inside of the report card envelope.

Retention

Retention should be considered on a case-by-case basis and only if the teacher and parents feel that it will benefit the child to repeat. Each child is unique and there are many factors that must be considered with the decision of holding a child back a year. Don't worry, this decision may be heavy but you will not have to carry it alone. You will always have the support and insight from your colleagues, administrators, and specialists. Together you will come to the right decision. Retention factors to consider are:

— Maturity or immaturity issues

— Does the child demonstrate coping skills?

— Is there a learning disability to consider?

— What score did they receive on the IQ test?

— How do the parents and administrators feel about retention?

— What type of social skills does the child possess?

— What is the child's age?

— Are there other children being promoted that function at the same aptitude level?

— Could the child qualify for beneficial services?

— Could interventions be established to help the child become successful?

— Would it benefit the child to be promoted this year and possibly be retained next year?

— What type of gap is the child demonstrating as compared to other below-average students?

— Are they stagnant in their learning or are they making some progress?

— Would the child benefit from summer school? Would they attend?

The Retention Process

When a teacher notices a serious academic lag in a student's learning behaviors, the child's name and concerns should be brought up for the teaming process or a teacher support meeting. During the team meeting, you and your colleagues will discuss your concerns and possible interventions.

Although you may have already brought up the child's name and stuck a little red flag next to it in October, January is the blossoming month for most students and that is when you will tend to notice their academic growth or lack thereof. January is the best time to bring up your retention concerns to the administration. Administrators will probably tell you to monitor the student's academics until February or March. In March you will more than likely meet to discuss the student's academic performance, compare their work samples to other low achievers in your class, and discuss the pros and cons of retention for the student.

If the possibility of retention is the consensus of the group, then the parent should be contacted by phone for a conference to discuss their child's academic performance as soon as possible. When conferencing with the parents, try to help them feel comfortable and approach the matter delicately. The parents' reaction may be to get frustrated, feel threatened (as if it is their fault), act as if they didn't notice a problem, say that they will "catch them up" over the summer, claim that the child has no problem doing academic tasks at home and they don't understand how this could be and go into denial, or they may just go with the flow. No matter what the parents' reaction, you must have proof in grades and work samples compared to other student work samples in the class. (Don't forget to cover the names of all work samples that you use for comparison purposes.)

To give the parent a glimpse of hope, tell them that if their child is able to perform on grade level by the end of the year that they will be promoted without any qualms. The parents should also understand that the teacher is the one who suggests retention but the parents actually have the final say as to whether or not their child will be retained. End the conference by telling the parents that you will keep them well informed on their child's progress and provide them with a letter which reiterates and documents the retention concerns you have for their child (see figure 8.8).

Figure 8.8
Example Retention Information Letter Written to Parents

Date

To the parents of _____,

    I have observed and documented concerns with _____'s first grade academic skills progress. _____ is performing at his personal best yet he is still unable to achieve the grade level standards in the areas of reading, writing, and math.

Reading:
  — Currently recognizes 11/26 lower case letters and 12/26 upper case letters.
  — Currently scored a 0% on a readiness level running record.
  — Currently recognizes 5 out of the 56 sight words.

Math:
  — Currently working toward identifying numerals 6 through 10.
  — Currently frustrates easily and lacks focus during math activities.
  — Currently unable to complete his math work independently. He relies heavily on a peer teacher or the teacher to guide him through completing his math activity.

Writing:
  — Currently working toward improving his fine motor skills or control of his pencil.
  — Currently needs to practice taking risks to begin stretch spelling or writing the sounds in words as he hears them in order to express himself on paper.

    Even with the extra learning support that _____ is receiving daily, he continues to struggle and demonstrate a large academic gap between him and his fellow classmates. To ensure that _____ will meet with academic success, he must perform at the expected first grade level by the end of the year in order to be suggested for promotion to second grade.

    Please feel free to contact me with any questions or concerns. I will be sure to keep you frequently informed on _____'s progress. Thank you for your support.

Sincerely,

(print name)

Conferences

Formal conference dates are scheduled according to your school district, however informal conferencing with parents will occur when requested by parents or the teacher throughout the school year.

Teacher Led Conferencing Tips

- Schedule formal conferences with parents by sending home a letter with their assigned conference time (see figure 8.9). If a parent has difficulty with their assigned time, then try to work around their schedule.

- For parents who can not meet with you in person, schedule a phone conference to discuss the student's progress.

- Before conferences begin, set up a desk outside of your classroom with a sign-in sheet. To help parents feel welcome, place a tablecloth over the desk and maybe add a small vase of flowers or offer a bowl of candy.

- Never conduct conferences from your desk. Sit at a table, such as your reading table, so the parents don't feel as if they are being talked down to.

- If the parent brings other siblings along, let them sit in your library center. Yes, your library will be a mess but that's what the library helpers are for the next day.

- Greet the parents with a smile, give them a handshake, and provide small talk to ease their apprehensiveness.

- Have the student's portfolio of work samples, the report card, the report card comments, and the completed conference outline (see figure 8.10) readily available for discussion. ★**Tip:** Make a copy of the conference outline for the parents to keep for their records.

- After greeting the parents, let them read their child's report card and comments independently. When the parent is done reading their child's report card, place the conference outline in a position on the table that can be seen by you and the parents. Use the conference outline as a guide for your discussion. Interject work samples from the portfolio to illustrate work habits, strengths, and areas of needed improvement.

Figure 8.9
Parent-Teacher Conference Information Letter

Conference Information Letter

Date

Dear _____,

    On *(scheduled date)*, *(name of your elementary school)* will be conducting parent-teacher conferences. Students will not attend school on this day so that the conferences may take place. Conferences will be held in fifteen-minute sessions, back to back. Your scheduled conference time is listed below. If for any reason you are not able to attend, then other arrangements can be made.

    During our parent-teacher conference we will discuss your child's academic progress, view work samples, and discuss any questions or concerns that you may have. Thank you for your participation and I look forward to meeting with you.

    Your scheduled conference time is on _____ at _____. Since conferences are scheduled one after another, please come on time and understand that there is a fifteen-minute session scheduled for each parent.

Sincerely,

(Teacher's Name)

Please detach and return this portion to school.

Student Name:
Guardian's Name:

☐   Yes, I will be able to attend the scheduled conference time on

_____ at _____.
      (date)   (time)

☐   No, I will not be able to attend the scheduled conference time. I would prefer to meet with you on the

date of _____ between the times of _____.

☐   Sorry, I will need to schedule a phone conference. Please call_____

@ _____ or _____ at your earliest convenience.

Figure 8.10
Conference Outline

Conference Outline

Date: _____   Time: _____

Student Name: _____

Parent Names: _____

Student's Overall Strengths:

Academic Progress in Reading:

Academic Progress in Math:

Academic Progress in Writing:

Areas of Needed Improvement:

Parent Comments:

Student Led Conferencing Tips

Student led conferences should be set up the same way a teacher led conference would be, the only difference is that the student will lead the discussion using the conference outline and the teacher interjects comments for support, guidance, and technical questions.

- Student led conferences are best for intermediate grades.
- Before a student led conference takes place, the teacher and student must discuss the purpose of the student leading the conference (to give the student responsibility and ownership of their learning). The student must also reflect on, complete, and practice, using the conference outline, with the teacher before the formal conference with the parents actually takes place.
- The student led conference may be new to most parents, therefore inform them about how the student led conference will unfold, the purpose for the student leading the conference, and the teacher's role.
- Impress upon your students and their parents how special this occasion is and that students are expected to dress nicely for the conference.

Dealing with Difficult Parents

Unfortunately one or two of your student's parents can be downright difficult to deal with. There are many possibilities for a parent's difficult behavior, such as personality, personal issues, stress, or misunderstandings. No matter how difficult a parent may be, never lose sight of the fact that you're in charge of what goes on in your classroom and even if it's your first year teaching, you know more about education than they do and you have the degree to prove it. Techniques for dealing with the difficult parent:

- Since the possibility of dealing with a difficult parent every year is high, do not exhaust yourself physically or emotionally on their issues.
- Don't give the parents a reason to judge your professionalism. Return phone calls, respond to notes, and schedule conferences in a timely manner.
- Always remain confident and calm when dealing with difficult parents.
- "I do acknowledge your concern" and "I'm sorry that you feel that way" are probably the best comebacks for items that the parent disagrees with, but neither you nor the school district plan to change anytime soon.
- If a parent gets unpredictable, irate, or uses profanity during a conference or discussion, tell them that you're sorry, but you will need to stop this discussion and continue it on a day that an administrator can also attend. Then report to the office as quickly as you can.
- Always leave your door open and tell a neighboring teacher to check on you frequently during your conference with a difficult parent. If the parent is a serious concern then request the presence of a mentor or administrator during the conference.

- For the parent who believes that you are the problem, not their child, bring in other teachers (special area teachers, speech pathologist, resource teacher) who have experienced the same issues which validate your concerns.
- Document and date any severe parent difficulties so that you are prepared for any situation. Administrators should be well informed of these difficulties.
- Always remain professional and kind; the parent may only want to get a rise out of you and if they are unsuccessful they will soon give up.
- Always remain strong and never let them see you cry.
- When you are scheduled to meet with a difficult parent, be prepared with notes, facts, dates, documentation, information, or examples on whatever the topic may be. (This is a good rule of thumb for any meeting that you attend.)

Planning Class Parties or Celebrations

Students get very excited when they are going to have a class party or celebration at school. Since parties are not related to academics and serve no educational purpose, most principals limit the amount of parties allowed to about two or three per year. Parties can't be taken away completely because after all, students are still children and they deserve a party here and there for all their hard work. The three most popular class parties are for the winter break, Valentine's Day, and the end of the year celebration; however, your principal will let you know which parties are appropriate. All parties or celebrations must be organized, so follow these suggestions to help make your class party an enjoyable experience:

- Be aware of and sensitive to the diverse beliefs of all parents and students. Refrain from giving your party a theme name that is directly related to a religion, and instead name the celebration with a generic theme, such as dubbing an Easter party as a *Spring Fling*. Also be very conscious of the fact that some people do not celebrate Halloween and they may associate dressing up in scary costumes with the celebration of the devil. Touchy, touchy.
- Plan your party for the designated day set by your school. The party should last for no more than thirty minutes and should take place an hour before dismissal. This schedule should give you thirty minutes to celebrate and thirty minutes to clean and pack up to go home.
- Request two or three large trash bags from the janitor ahead of time.
- Send a note home one week in advance that informs parents of the purpose for the celebration, the date, times, donations needed, and volunteer information (see figure 8.11).
- For Valentine's Day, don't forget to send home a list of student first names and last name initials. No student phone numbers or personal information should be included on the list.

- Utilize parent volunteers by having them distribute paper goods, food, and drinks, and by having them set up and clean up. While parents set up and clean up, the teacher should read a story to the students related to the holiday celebration.
- Do not let students walk around while eating. Ask parent volunteers to do refills on food and drinks. Students must stay seated and talk to friends that they sit near due to the possibility of someone choking on their food.
- Set a time limit for food to be eaten and anything they don't finish eating should be taken home in a gallon-size baggie or must be thrown away.
- Monitor the noise and activity levels. Although it is a party, appropriate behavior is expected and behavior management is a must.

Figure 8.11
Classroom Parties
Examples of Parent Information Letters

Winter Celebration Information

Dear Parents,

On *(date of celebration)* we have scheduled our winter celebration from 2:30 to 3:00. We will celebrate the winter holiday with cookies and juice. As we eat we will enjoy a few good books. If you would like to volunteer to read to the students during our celebration time frame, please let me know.

If possible, we are asking each student to donate the item that has been circled on their information sheet. Thank you in advance for your gracious donations!

Holiday Cookies

Candy Canes – one pack of twelve

Juice Boxes – one pack of twelve

Paper Plates – one pack

Napkins – one pack

Valentine's Day Celebration

Dear Parents,

On *(date of celebration)* we will celebrate Valentine's Day from 2:30 to 3:00. We will celebrate our happiness and friendships by bringing in Valentines to distribute, making a Valentine's Day craft, and enjoying a bag of chips and juice while reading our Valentine's Day cards. A list of student names has been attached. If you would like to volunteer during our Valentine celebration time frame, please let me know.

If possible, we are asking each student to donate the item that has been circled on their information sheet. Thank you for your help!

One Pack of Red Construction Paper

Juice Boxes – one pack of twelve

One Box of Snack Size Potato Chips

Napkins – one pack

Surviving American Education Week

"As if my room is even big enough for the thirty students, desks, and chairs assigned to it, why not throw in thirty sets of parents, and folding chairs to boot," said the disgruntled teacher. Ahhh, this sounds like one of the many joys of American Education Week, but don't worry, you survived the first week of school and you will survive American Education Week too.

American Education Week was established so that the parents of school children nationwide could observe and share in their child's educational experience. To ensure a great experience for everyone, follow these tips:

- Have students write a letter to their parents inviting them to attend American Education Week.
- Send home an American Education Week information letter (which could be attached to the invitation that the students wrote to their parents) that states the designated days, times, room number, directions to your classroom from within the building, the daily class schedule, and any requests (turn off all cell phones, no food or drink, please do not allow your child to sit on your lap during learning activities, etc.).
- Hang a visible welcome sign that gives the teacher's name, grade, and room number.
- Provide a desk outside of your room with a sign-in sheet (refer to figure 8.1) and pens. You may also want to place a small sign that reminds parents to turn off their cell phones.
- Dress professionally this week, as you should every week.
- Get to school early to prepare lessons and manipulatives.
- Do not change your teaching routine or behavior management strategies. The parents are in your classroom to observe a day in the life of their child, so keep it as close to normal as possible. Not to mention, if the student's routine is changed then they will question it and, depending on their age, they may get confused or frustrated.
- Be yourself and don't hesitate to reprimand students just because their parents are in the room. Maintain control at all times.

Chapter 9
Methods for Teaching Reading Groups and Managing Centers

Teaching a child how to read will be the most challenging, yet rewarding job responsibility that a teacher will have. In this chapter you will have access to methods to administer a basic running record, assess your student's reading level, establish and teach reading strategies, manage reading group rotations, design unique and age-appropriate centers, and understand how to assign centers and seatwork activities.

Administering Running Records

A running record is an assessment tool that will document student reading progress and help you to group students into diagnostic reading groups according to their reading abilities. Running records identify individual student reading levels by analyzing their ability to read a leveled text.

Example of a Completed Running Record

Student Name: _____   Date:_____

The Cat Sat
Pre-Primer Level

✓   ✓ ✓ <u>in</u> ✓ ✓ <u>rug</u>
The cat sat <u>on</u> the blue <u>mat.</u>   **34 words** = 66 % = **Hard**
                                           10 errors

✓   ✓ ✓ <u>in</u> ✓ ✓snow✓
The cat sat <u>on</u> the red ^hat.

✓   ✓ ✓ <u>in</u> ✓ <u>black</u> <u>wat</u>
The cat sat on the brown vat.

✓   ✓ ✓ <u>in</u> ✓ <u>—</u> ✓
The cat sat on the gray rat.

✓   ✓ ✓ in ✓ legs / SC
The cat sat on Pat's <u>lap.</u>

Utilizing running records in the classroom:

1. Familiarize yourself with the scoring marks.

<table>
<tr><td colspan="3" align="center"><u>**Running Record Scoring Marks**</u></td></tr>
<tr><td>**Scoring Marks**</td><td>**Definition of Scoring Marks**</td><td align="center">**Example**</td></tr>
<tr><td align="center">✓</td><td>Read word correctly</td><td align="center">✓ ✓ ✓
The bear ran.</td></tr>
<tr><td align="center">_____</td><td>Omitted the word</td><td align="center">✓ — ✓
The bear ran.</td></tr>
<tr><td align="center">⋀</td><td>Inserted a word</td><td align="center">✓ big ✓ ✓
The ^ bear ran.</td></tr>
<tr><td align="center">/ sc</td><td>Self corrected/not an error</td><td align="center">✓ baby/sc ✓
The bear ran.</td></tr>
<tr><td align="center">b¯</td><td>Recognized first sound only</td><td align="center">✓ b- ✓
The bear ran.</td></tr>
<tr><td align="center">↓⌐R 2</td><td>Repeated a line or word and the # of times it was repeated. Not considered an error.</td><td align="center">↓The bear ran. R1</td></tr>
<tr><td align="center">*Write incorrect word Over the correct word*</td><td>Read incorrect word</td><td align="center">✓ baby ✓
The b̄ēār ran.</td></tr>
</table>

2. Choose a range of books that your school has to offer to perform running record assessments which have been leveled according to their readability. The reading series that your school has chosen to implement may include a leveling system for their book titles.

3. Create a running record recording sheet for the range of leveled books that you have chosen by typing the title, reading level of the text, and the words directly from the text (only 100 words or less). Place five spaces between each sentence so that you have adequate space for writing the scoring marks. Some reading series may provide running record sheets for some or all book titles.

4. Complete running records with a few students per day until you have finally met with the entire class. Assessing students with running records should occur at the beginning of the first quarter and at the end of the first through fourth quarters. Times that are best for assessing a student would be before announcements, before conducting a guided reading group, and/or after conducting a guided reading group.

5. Introduce the title of the book and allow the student to take a picture walk before beginning the running record. When assessing a student with a running record it should always be a *cold* read. *Cold*, when referring to reading, means the student is not familiar with the text and the teacher has not prompted or given any support to the student as they read.

6. Direct the student to read the text as you write the running record scoring marks above each word as they read, omit, repeat, or demonstrate an error. IMPORTANT: The purpose of a running record is to find out the student's instructional reading level, therefore do not assist the students as they read. If the student has a question about the text, just tell them to use their reading strategies and to do their best.

7. If the student is very fluent and you are having difficulty keeping up with the scoring marks as the student reads, then ask the student to pause for a moment so that you may catch up.

8. When the student is done reading, ask them to reflect on verbal comprehension questions about the text. Next, discuss the errors that were made and the reading strategies that could be used to help the student overcome making the same types of errors again.

9. Make any teacher observation notes directly on the running record recording sheet (e.g., fluent, not fluent, used voice inflection, monotone, did not yield to punctuation marks, relied heavily on picture clues, did or did not comprehend what was read, read too fast, wasn't focused).

10. Use the running records conversion table shown in figure 9.1 to calculate the student's running record score to find their current instructional reading level. If necessary, round the score up; for instance, a score of 3.5 would actually read as a score of 4. If a student is reading a leveled book and scores in the Easy or Frustrated range, then the book that they are reading is not on their reading level. Continue the running record process with other leveled books until they score Instructional and only then can you properly identify their reading level.

Calculating running record scores:

● Divide the number of words read by the number of errors to find the error rate.

$$\frac{\text{\# of words}}{\text{\# of errors}}$$

● Locate the error rate on the conversion table and its corresponding percentage, then identify the reading level. Group the students according to their current reading abilities for the purpose of conducting guided reading groups.

Figure 9.1

Conversion Table for Running Record Scores		
$\dfrac{\text{\# of words}}{\text{\# of errors}}$		
Error Rate	**Corresponding Percent %**	**Reading Level**
1: 200	99.5	
1: 100	99	
1: 50	98	Easy = 95-100%
1: 35	97	
1: 25	96	
1: 20	95	
1: 17	94	
1: 14	93	
1: 12.5	92	Instructional = 90-94%
1: 11.75	91	
1: 10	90	
1: 9	89	
1: 8	87.5	
1: 7	85.5	
1: 6	83	
1: 5	80	Hard = 80-89%
1: 4	75	
1: 3	66	
1: 2	50	

Reading Strategies

Reading strategies are cues that students should become familiar with and utilize when trying to decode unfamiliar words. The reading strategies should be memorized by the students and briefly reviewed on a daily basis before students attempt to read the text independently. Each school or school district should have a universal set of reading strategies for the students to reference. If your school does not have a standard set of reading strategies in place then enlarge the following poster shown in figure 9.2.

Figure 9.2
Reading Strategies Poster

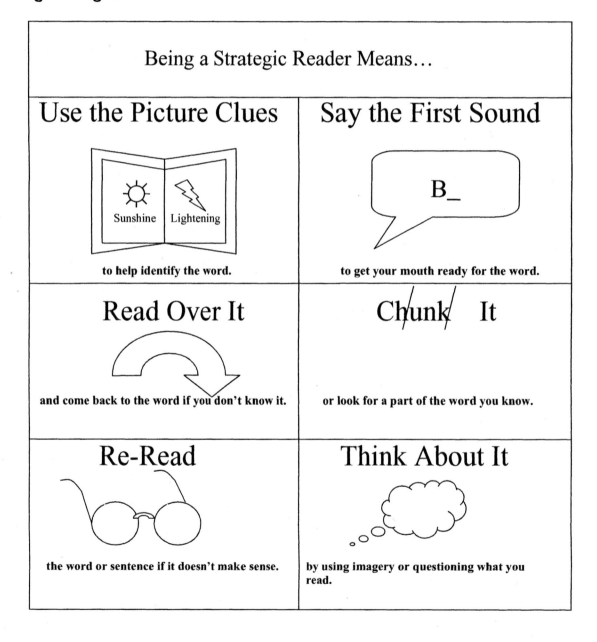

How to Teach Reading

Learning to read is an individualized process which happens for students as they are developmentally ready. The developmentally appropriate stages for learning to read are:

Grades K-2 Learning to Read (decoding)

Grades 3-5 Reading to Learn (comprehension)

However, these stages are not set in stone since within each class for grades K-5 there will be a range of readers from readiness to fluent, and the teacher must meet all of the students' needs by forming guided reading groups.

Guided reading groups provide direct instruction that is designed to motivate and support all students as they strive to become independent readers. Guided reading groups are composed of homogeneously grouped students based on student running record scores (the amount of reading groups that you divide students into is based on class needs) and all groups must receive direct reading instruction on a daily basis (see page 178 for suggested time frames for meeting with each reading group). Most importantly the reading groups must be fluid, meaning students must be reevaluated informally through teacher observation or with running records each quarter and regrouped according to their current reading abilities.

Once the teacher has completed running records and grouped the students homogeneously according to their reading abilities, the next step is to plan for direct reading instruction. To do so use the *Before, During,* and *After Reading* planning grid shown in figure 9.3. How to utilize the reading planning grid:

1. Decide on a formative assessment and appropriate reading books which will match your state and district curriculum indicators and objective.

2. Before allowing students to read while in guided reading groups prepare them for the text by choosing one or two *Before* reading activities and coaching prompts listed on the planning grid.

3. As the students read, select and implement *During* reading activities and coaching prompts that match your lesson objective and best suit your needs for teaching comprehension of the text.

4. Once students have completed their reading assignment, utilize the *After* reading activities and coaching prompts that best suit your teaching needs.

Figure 9.3

The Before, During, and After Planning Grid for Teaching Reading
■ = must be implemented   ● = may be implemented

Formative Assessments (choose one)	●KWL Chart ●The Decision Tree ●Vocabulary Activity	●Main Idea Table ●Writing Prompt ●Journal Entry	●Idea Web ●Write a List ●Read and Respond to Questions	●Venn Diagram ●T Chart ●Story Map	●Sequence Chain ●Beginning, Middle, and End Event Chart	●Problem/ Solution ●Cause/ Effect
Before Reading Activities	●Identify background knowledge. ●Connect student's lives or knowledge to the text.	●Identify the text features and format. ●Discuss the objective and incorporate a mini lesson.	●Make predictions by analyzing the cover, title, illustrations, and/or the text.	●Take a picture walk and discuss what you see. ●Review new vocabulary words within the text by framing.	●Recall events or information if students are revisiting the text.	●Set a purpose for reading: "Today we will read to find out _____."
Before Reading Coaching Prompts	■Review reading strategies. ■Introduce or review the vocabulary.					
During Reading Activities	■Distribute reading tools (headphones, phonic phones, and/or pointers). ■Read silently, buddy read, whisper read, popcorn read, and/or choral read the assigned pages.	●Ask: What do you think the author meant by _____? ●Ask: Think about and question what you read.	●Check predictions as you read. ●Make more predictions by asking questions like: What do you think will happen next and why?	●Visualize and describe what you read. ●Stop students periodically to question them on what they read (comprehension).	●Summarize what you read. ●Recall who, what, when, where, why, and how.	●Take notes about _____. ●Use sticky notes to mark text where you can identify _____.
During Reading Coaching Prompts	■Monitor fluency, directionality, voice inflection, and the use of reading strategies.	●Get your mouth ready for the first sound. ●Look at the picture clue.	●Does the word you just said make sense in that sentence? What would? ●Re-read.	●Read what you see. ●If student says the incorrect word, ask: Does that look right?	●Chunk it, look for the part of the word you know. ●Read over it and come back to it.	●Think about it, make a picture in your mind.
After Reading Coaching Prompts	●Praise students for using their reading strategies by giving examples such as: "I like how John (insert a strategy)."	●Conduct a group discussion on comprehension.	●Check the purpose that was set for reading.			
After Reading Activities	■Review and practice the lesson's objective and assign the seatwork activity.	●Connect student's lives and background knowledge to the text.	●Review the vocabulary.	●Discuss whether the students liked or disliked what they read and why.	●Recall details or sequence events.	●Revisit the text to answer questions verbally or written.

Building Vocabulary

Building vocabulary can be done by providing students with many opportunities to see, say, and write the words they need to know in order to be successful. Building your student's sight vocabulary list doesn't have to be rote and boring—there are many fun ways to introduce and work on vocabulary, such as:

Pocket Words:

1. Write three to five new vocabulary words on index cards and secure them together on an O-ring (typically called a word ring) that students can carry around in their pocket or hook to their belt loop.

2. As the students carry these words around with them throughout the day, the student's teacher, special area teachers, and administration can ask them to read the words for practice.

Cut-Up Sentences:

1. The teacher provides the child with a strip of paper displaying a written sentence that includes words the student knows and the new vocabulary words they have been practicing.

2. The student should first read the sentence and identify the new vocabulary words.

3. Next, the student will cut the sentence strip between each word in order to make small word cards.

4. Then, the student will mix the word cards up and practice reading each word individually.

5. Finally, the student will put the words in order to recreate the original sentence. Another option is to require the student to glue the sentence back in order at the top of a piece of lined paper and then ask them to rewrite and illustrate the sentence.

Wordo:

1. Create a tic-tac-toe board for each student.

2. Tell students to write the given vocabulary words in random boxes on the tic-tac-toe board (if there are less than nine vocabulary words they can write chosen words more than once until their board is full).

3. Once each square on the student's Wordo board is full, pass out nine pennies to each child.

4. The teacher will call out random vocabulary words and the student should cover the words on his or her Wordo board with a penny as they are said.

5. The first to get three pennies in a row calls out "WORDO" and wins a sticker.

Word Cover-Up:

1. Cover the vocabulary word within a sentence (a sentence within a book's text or written on a sentence strip) with a small sticky note.

2. Have the students select the vocabulary word they have learned that would make sense in the sentence where the sticky note has been placed by saying the word orally, writing the word on a wipe board, or by rewriting the sentence using the correct vocabulary word.

Wipe Board Practice:

1. Students say and write the given vocabulary word.

2. Students write the vocabulary word which would make sense in the verbal sentence given by the teacher.

3. Students look up the vocabulary word in the text and then write the word and page number they found it on.

Highlighting Words:

1. Students can find the vocabulary words in the text using highlighting tape or sticky notes.

2. Next, the student could record the page that the vocabulary word was found on or write the sentence that uses the word. Another option is to type a paragraph for the students by incorporating the vocabulary words and instruct the student to use a highlighter, or a yellow crayon, to highlight the appropriate vocabulary words.

Word Hunt:

1. Students can frame the vocabulary word (put one index finger in front of and one index finger in back of the word) found in the text.

2. Motivate students to find vocabulary words using pointers or word finders such as bubble blowing wands from discarded bubble bottles, index cards with a small word-sized rectangle cut out of the center, plastic stir sticks (typically used for mixing drinks), sticky notes, or decorated popsicle sticks.

Cloze Sentences:

1. Students can complete sentences by choosing the appropriate vocabulary word from a given word box.

2. To go a step further, students could illustrate each sentence.

Building Fluency

Building fluency is necessary for students to better comprehend what they have read. The following strategies will help to build your student's reading fluency:

- Introduce, define, and use the word *fluency* with students beginning as early as kindergarten.
- Tap a pencil as the student reads and challenge them to read the words at the same pace of the tapping that they hear.
- Tape record students as they read a text selection and have them rate their own fluency on a scale of 1-5 or have students "buddy read" and require students to rate their partner's reading fluency on a scale of 1-5.
- All teachers should model fluency and voice inflection by reading aloud to the class as frequently as possible and on a daily basis.
- Teach students how to self monitor their fluency by instructing them to tap their foot at a fluency rate they wish to read at and challenge them to read a word each time their foot taps in order to pick up their reading pace.
- Silent fluency can be tested by assigning pages to be read and a time limit for reading those pages. Test student fluency by their ability to read and comprehend the assigned text.

Building Comprehension Skills

Once students have begun to master reading, the next step is for the student to understand what they have read by building their comprehension skills. The following are ways to help make that connection between learning to read and reading to learn:

- Connect the text to the student's life by providing pictures, physical objects, or examples of the text's topic.
- Create comprehension word cards using index cards that state Who, What, When, Where, Why, and How. After the student reads a part of the text, show a comprehension word card for the student to answer based on what they have read.
- Purchase a beach ball and on each color panel of the ball, write one of the following questions:
  — Who were the characters?
  — Where is the setting?
  — What is the problem?
  — What is the solution?
  — What happened at the beginning?
  — What happened in the middle?
  — What happened at the end?
  — What was your favorite part and why?

Toss the beach ball to a student and whatever color panel their right thumb touches is the question they must answer.

- Sticky notes can be a reading teacher's best friend. Depending on the focus for reading, write the following on sticky notes and provide enough for each student:
  — main character

  — setting

  — problem

  — solution

  — beginning event

  — middle event

  — end event

As the student reads, have him or her mark the text with the appropriately labeled sticky note. For seatwork, students could refer to the sticky notes to answer questions or to reflect on their reading.

- Create a story wheel by cutting a circle from tag board and dividing it into fourths. In each divided section write a comprehension question. Place a spinner in the center of the wheel by cutting an arrow from the tag board and fastening it to the wheel with a paper fastener or brad. Students can take turns spinning the arrow and whichever comprehension question the arrow lands on the student should answer it. Many story wheels could be made and students could use them with a partner to practice answering comprehension questions with one another. **★Tip:** Add picture clues for primary students.

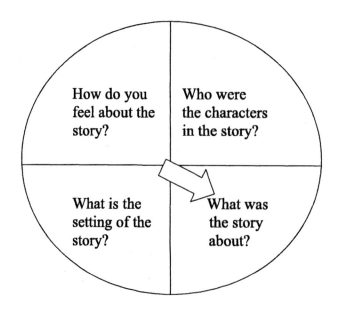

● Pinch cards are another fun way to build your student's comprehension skills. Pinch cards are made by using index cards in the vertical position that have been divided with lines which have been drawn for displaying different comprehension questions. The idea is for the student to pinch with their thumb and index finger on the comprehension question they would like to attempt to answer. Students could use the pinch cards to answer questions in group or independent situations. ★**Tip:** Add picture clues for primary students.

Who?
What?
When?
Where?
Why?
How?

The Guided Reading Group Rotation Chart

How do you plan to herd your students about the room as they rotate between guided reading groups, centers, and seatwork? Easy, create a group rotation chart and a signal (hand clap or ringing a bell) to manage student movement between work areas. It may take about three to six weeks of walking the students through their rotations before they are able to do so independently.

Students should work in their assigned work area and not be allowed to move about the room. Any student who does not stay in their group's assigned area and complete the necessary activity should instead sit within close proximity of the teacher until the next rotation begins. Follow these steps to move your groups from reading, centers, and seatwork activities:

- Make a rotation chart large enough for all students to see (refer to figures 9.4 and 9.5).
- Decide how long each group will work before each rotation and set a timer to stay on track. The following is a list of time frame examples:
  — Pre-kindergarten and kindergarten groups last 15 to 20 minutes each.
    (15-20 minutes at reading, 15-20 minutes at seatwork, 15-20 minutes at centers)

  — First through second grade groups last 25 to 30 minutes each.
    (25-30 minutes at reading, 25-30 minutes at seatwork, 25-30 minutes at centers)

  — Third through fifth grade groups last 30 to 35 minutes each.
    (30 minutes at reading, 30 minutes at seatwork/centers, 30 minutes whole group activity)

- Give each reading group a name (color words work best for organizing center assignments) so that each group knows where to be for each rotation.
- Establish a signal to let students know when to rotate (hand clap, ringing a bell, etc.).
- Walk your students through the rotation procedure every day for as long as necessary before expecting them to find their rotating work areas independently. Depending on your students, this routine may take three to six weeks to master.

Figure 9.4
Rotation Chart for Three Guided Reading Groups

	First Rotation	Second Rotation	Third Rotation
Red Group:	Reading ⟹	Seatwork ⟹	Centers
Blue Group:	Seatwork ⟹	Centers ⟹	Reading
Green Group:	Centers ⟹	Reading ⟹	Seatwork

Figure 9.5
Rotation Chart for Two Guided Reading Groups

	First Rotation	Second Rotation
Red Group:	Reading ⟹	Seatwork/Centers
Blue Group:	Seatwork/Centers ⟹	Reading

Understanding Centers

Centers are a very important part of a primary classroom. Centers give a group of students the opportunity to work independently or within cooperative groups to complete hands-on learning activities and communicate ideas and explore concepts.

Centers are utilized in classrooms from pre-kindergarten to, usually, second grade. Primary grades typically teach three guided reading groups on a daily basis. Students are assessed with running records or a vocabulary list and grouped according to their reading abilities, ranging from above average, average, and below. Simultaneously, one group of students is working in centers, the second group of students will be working at their desk doing a vocabulary or comprehension seatwork activity, and the third group will be working with the teacher on guided reading activities. Each group will rotate to all of these work areas at a predetermined time decided by the teacher.

Intermediate grades usually teach two guided reading groups on a daily basis. Students are grouped according to their reading capabilities. While one group is working with the teacher in a guided reading group, the other group will be working at their desks doing seatwork activities consisting of an independent reading of the text and a vocabulary or comprehension task. If the student finishes their seatwork activity early they may choose or visit their assigned center. Intermediate centers usually consist of a classroom library, math worksheets or games, and a computer station. To find out how many centers you will need to establish, complete the following formula:

1. Decide how many centers you will need by dividing your students into diagnostic reading groups.

2. Calculate your center to student ratio needs based on the reading group with the largest amount of students. Divide the amount of students that are in your largest reading group by two (since only two students at a time are allowed in a center).

3. If you are able to divide evenly, then create the necessary even amount of centers calculated. If you are not able to divide evenly, then add an extra center and one student will work alone within a center.

4. Now that you know how many centers are needed to accommodate your students, you can begin to set up and design the center activities based on your student and curriculum needs.

Center Activity Ideas

Center activities can be changed on a weekly, bi-weekly, or monthly basis throughout the academic year to match the curriculum and student needs. All centers should have written directions posted in a visible area that explain (using kid-friendly language) how to perform the task the student is responsible for completing during their center time.

The following four staple centers are commonly used year round by only changing the activity as necessary:

- *Classroom Library:* A quiet reading area in the primary and intermediate classroom where students have access to current reading materials which have been organized for easy access according to themes or topics. Students can choose to read books quietly to themselves, stuffed animals, or a buddy. Other activities could include making bookmarks, publishing books, and demonstrating comprehension skills by writing and drawing about a story they have read. ★**Tip:** Post a map of the world on the wall next to the library for students to find the places they are reading about. Organization for this center is mentioned earlier in this chapter.

- *Writing Center:* Students are able to explore and extend their writing abilities by using pens, pencils, markers, crayons, stationery, lined paper, envelopes, index cards, construction paper, stamps, stickers, stencils, writing prompts, and a children's dictionary. Organize this center with a system containing drawers that are labeled as to which supply it contains. To enhance your writing center, add a mailbox for students to write and send letters to one another. The teacher can pass the letters out at the end of the day along with other papers that need to go home.

- *Listening Center:* Set up a tent with lots of windows (for student monitoring purposes) or a cozy corner with large pillows for students to enjoy stories by listening to books on tape which have been purchased or recorded by the teacher. The books on tape demonstrate how to read stories with fluency and voice inflection. Provide pencils, clipboards, blank paper for student reflections, and a comprehension activity related to the story on tape for students to complete.

- *Computer Center:* All classrooms today should have an area designated to provide students with exposure of technology. Computers in the classroom are necessary for practice with manipulating the mouse and cursor, keyboarding skills, and navigating the Internet. Be sure to provide headphones for each computer to eliminate noise distractions. It is very important that you choose computer software that has been approved by your school district. Check with your school's librarian or technology liaison in order to receive a list of approved computer software.

If more centers are needed, the following can be implemented according to your students' needs and interests. These centers can include, but are not limited to:

- *Reading the Room/Writing the Room:* Provide a fun variety of pointers such as wands, batons, garden gloves to wear and point with, flashlights, and a flyswatter with a rectangular hole cut out of the center to motivate students to read words around the room. For writing around the room, include two small spiral notebooks with pens tied to them for students to be able to print words they see around the room.

- *Art Center:* In this center, students can reflect creatively on what they have learned during recent subject activities. Students can also complete art projects by using their imagination or by following a set of written directions with picture clues in order to read to perform a task. Provide a plastic drawer system for organization that has been labeled to contain a variety of craft supplies for students to manipulate and use for making their masterpiece.

- *Math Center:* Provide students with a fun, hands-on math-related activity or game. An activity sheet or blank paper should be provided for students to write about what they have accomplished while working at their center. A few teacher-created activities could include puzzles, measuring, matching, sorting, adding, subtracting, or making patterns with string and beads. Purchased board games related to math concepts could also be made available for student engagement.

- *Science Center:* Students can conduct experiments by making and exploring a hypothesis to a given question. Provide students with science materials necessary for the experiment, pencils, and data recording sheets. Motivate students by including lab coats (or white button-up shirts in a large adult size), rubber dish washing gloves, and safety glasses for students to wear as they work.

- *Overhead Projector Center:* Place the overhead projector on the ground in front of a wall with plenty of empty space so that students can project images of words and sentences they have built. Provide students with a large baggie containing plastic alphabet letters or transparency letter tiles for making words. Also have available overhead pens and transparencies of lined paper for students to practice handwriting. To help students with writing ideas, include a basket containing books that are currently being read during guided reading groups and a children's dictionary.

- *Pocket Chart:* Students can use the pocket chart and manipulatives to make words or sentences, sequence story events, and to complete matching activities. Provide markers, sentence strips, and scissors for students to create their own pocket chart words and sentences.

- *Flannel Board:* Students can manipulate the flannel board picture pieces to retell or create stories. Flannel letters can also be used to make names, words, and sentences. Provide paper, color pencils, and pens for students to write stories about the flannel pieces they have arranged.

- *Reading to Perform a Task:* Written step-by-step directions with picture clues for completing a multistep task and materials necessary for completing this task should be provided. The reading to perform a task should be related to a theme or unit that the class is studying.

- *Alphabet Center:* Students could manipulate magnetic letters on cookie sheets in order to make words, make letters by molding clay, cut up magazines to match pictures to letter sounds, practice writing letters on a chalkboard, glue cereal pieces onto construction paper in the formation of letters, or use alphabet stamps to practice stamping words.

A pre-kindergarten and kindergarten class may include the centers listed below:

- *Sand and Water Table:* Provide two chairs for students to sit on while working in the sand and water area. Students can share ideas and explore with sand and water tools such as water wheels, float and sink objects, scoops, funnels, molds, buckets, sifters, and rakes. Structured activities can include writing letters, names, and words in the sand, comparing sizes of objects, exploring capacities, and other early childhood activities. ★**Tip:** Beans, rice, and dry pasta could also be used as other options to fill the sand and water tubs for measurement, sorting, and counting activities. Provide plastic smocks to protect the students' clothing while participating in the water and sand activities.

- *Small Blocks and Hollow Blocks:* Display a written task for students to construct with blocks. For example, students could be assigned to build the setting of a story as a reading activity or a fire truck if they are studying a unit on fire safety. Provide students with books related to the theme of their building block task. Also provide a bin with pencils, pens, and clipboards for students to draw and write about what they have built or what they would like to build with the blocks.

- *Housekeeping:* In housekeeping, students will develop social skills, role play, read books related to the home, and write grocery lists or letters to friends and family members. Provide materials such as plastic food, plastic utensils and plates, a cordless phone, dishrags, a plastic plant, multicultural dolls, a stuffed dog, a dog bowl, a plastic vase containing artificial flowers, a child-size table and chair set, a tablecloth, a housekeeping sink set, menus, a phone book, a flyer with grocery store advertisements, coupons, pens, paper, and books related to topics of the home.

- *Puppet Theatre:* Students use puppets to reenact story events, create skits, and demonstrate comprehension skills. Provide paper, pencils, crayons, and clipboards for students to write about the story they have reenacted with the puppets.

Unique Furniture for Centers

To make your centers inviting, be creative with the furniture that you choose. Unconventional furniture is a wonderful way to save space in your classroom and it motivates students to learn by adding a little fun to your centers. There are many possibilities for classroom furniture. Use the following examples to help spark your imagination:

- A children's plastic picnic table would be a great furniture choice for a math or art center.
- A tent, with lots of large windows for keeping an eye on student activity, can become a fun listening center.
- A plastic tablecloth placed over two desks is a wonderful "reading to perform a task" center.
- Two bean bags and clipboards could be a functional writing center.
- Small foldable beach chairs or large throw pillows placed in the library center lend themselves as relaxing places to sit and read books. This type of seating can also be easily tucked away.
- Carpet squares are portable and can be used as seats while students complete math or flannel board activities.
- An overturned plastic milk crate or bucket could serve as a small table or place a square pillow on top of the overturned crate to use as a make-shift seat.
- Blow-up chairs, rocking chairs, or a bench could be used as creative children's seats.
- Bar stools that have a high back for support as the student sits or stools with shortened legs can be an exciting seat for the student to sit on as they share their work or a story with the class.
- Oversized and overstuffed chairs could also be a great furniture choice if you place a plastic covering over the chair to protect against the spread of lice.
- A child-sized table and chair set with a beach umbrella, a small air mattress, seat cushions, or a bathtub with pillows inside could serve as a great reading area.

Center Sacks – The Alternative to Stationary Centers

Center sacks provide a great alternative to stationary centers that use valuable space with bulky tables and chairs. A center sack is simply a tote or book bag which contains center activities. Each student may choose a center sack and find a quiet space to complete the included activity. To establish center sacks you will need to:

1. Purchase the necessary amount of tote bags or small book bags (based on the number of students in your largest reading group divided by two).

2. Develop and insert the center sack activities (see examples listed below).

3. Along with the center sack activities, include a towel or solid color place mat to serve as a work area for the students.

4. Display the bags in an easily accessible area with a small coat rack, a hook system that you have established on a wall or underneath the chalkboard, or by storing the bags in a large plastic bin.

5. Include a baggie which contains the supplies needed to complete the center sack activity.

Center Sack Activity Ideas

- *Math:* Within the sack place math-related games, books, or activities and, if necessary, a baggie containing paper, pencil, and crayons.

- *Reading and Responding to Books:* Provide a bag with a variety of stories, puppets, pencils, crayons, paper, or a book critique activity.

- *Reading and Writing the Room:* Include pointers for students to read words around the room, two spiral notebooks, and a baggie containing a pen, pencil, and markers within a tote bag.

- *Writing:* Place lined paper, plain paper, construction paper, stationery, index cards, envelopes, and a baggie containing a pen, pencil, color pencils, stamps, and stickers in a sack for student use.

- *Reading to Perform a Task:* A laminated step-by-step task and a baggie with materials necessary to perform the task. Books can also be included that are related to the task topic.

- *Art:* Provide a bag with children's *How-To* craft books and baggies with a variety of arts and craft supplies along with a pencil box containing glue, a pencil, pen, crayons, and an eraser.

- *Making Words:* Place a small cookie sheet to manipulate magnetic letters into words, clay for making letters and words, a children's dictionary for reference, alphabet letter stamps, paper, and pencils in a center sack.

- *Listening:* Insert a portable handheld cassette player with headphones, book on tape materials, an activity sheet, and a baggie containing a pencil, crayons, and paper in a tote bag for students to use.

Assigning Centers

Okay, now you know how to rotate the groups of students from their reading group, to centers, and to their seatwork areas. But there is still one remaining question: When a group is assigned to work in centers, how do they each know where to go? The answer: Create a center chart which will give students a choice as to which center they will attend, or create a center chart that assigns students to specific centers for the day.

Free Choice Center Chart

A free choice center chart allows students to decide what center they will attend during their group's turn for center work activities. To create a free choice environment you can use a *Center Sign-Up Chart* (figure 9.6) and/or a center contract (figure 9.7). Just as a word of warning: If you opt to have free choice centers, then make certain that your class can handle the responsibilities that go along with this freedom. Students who can not follow the center rules that you establish should be removed from the center and placed in time-out either at their seat or next to the teacher. High expectations are necessary for center time to be productive. To use a *Center Sign-Up Chart* you will need to follow these steps:

1. Create a chart with icons representing the centers that are available to choose from in your room. To make the center icon cards interchangeable, place Velcro on the back of each card and on the poster where they will be displayed. Make your poster long and horizontal with the center icons placed close to the bottom. Setting the chart up this way will enable students to easily clip their clothespin onto the chart (refer to figure 9.6). ★**Tip:** Remember to add picture clues to help the struggling readers understand the center contract or center chart.

2. Buy clothespins and label them with student names. Name each reading group with a color word. Use marker, color sticker dots, or spray paint to mark each student's clothespin in order to coordinate with their assigned reading group color. Students will find their clothespin and clip it onto the center they would like to choose for the day.

3. Allow students to sign up for centers in the morning before announcements begin. Students should understand that only two students may be in one center at a given time, so that means only two of the same color clothespins can be clipped beside one another under the same center icon at a time.

Figure 9.6
Center Sign-Up Chart

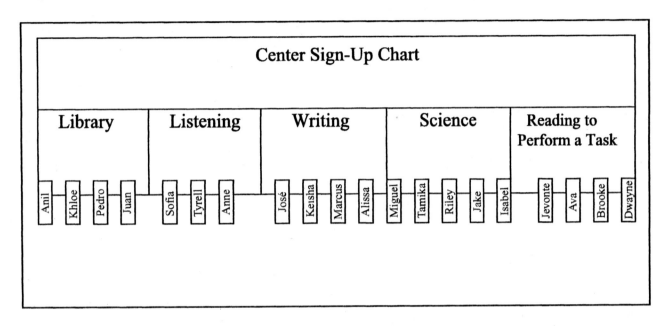

Center Contract

To implement free choice centers, students are responsible for documenting the center that they visit each day. If students visit a different center every day, then their contract should be complete by the end of the week. Design your center contract so that it meets the needs of the children in your class and matches the centers offered around your room.

Figure 9.7
Center Contract Example

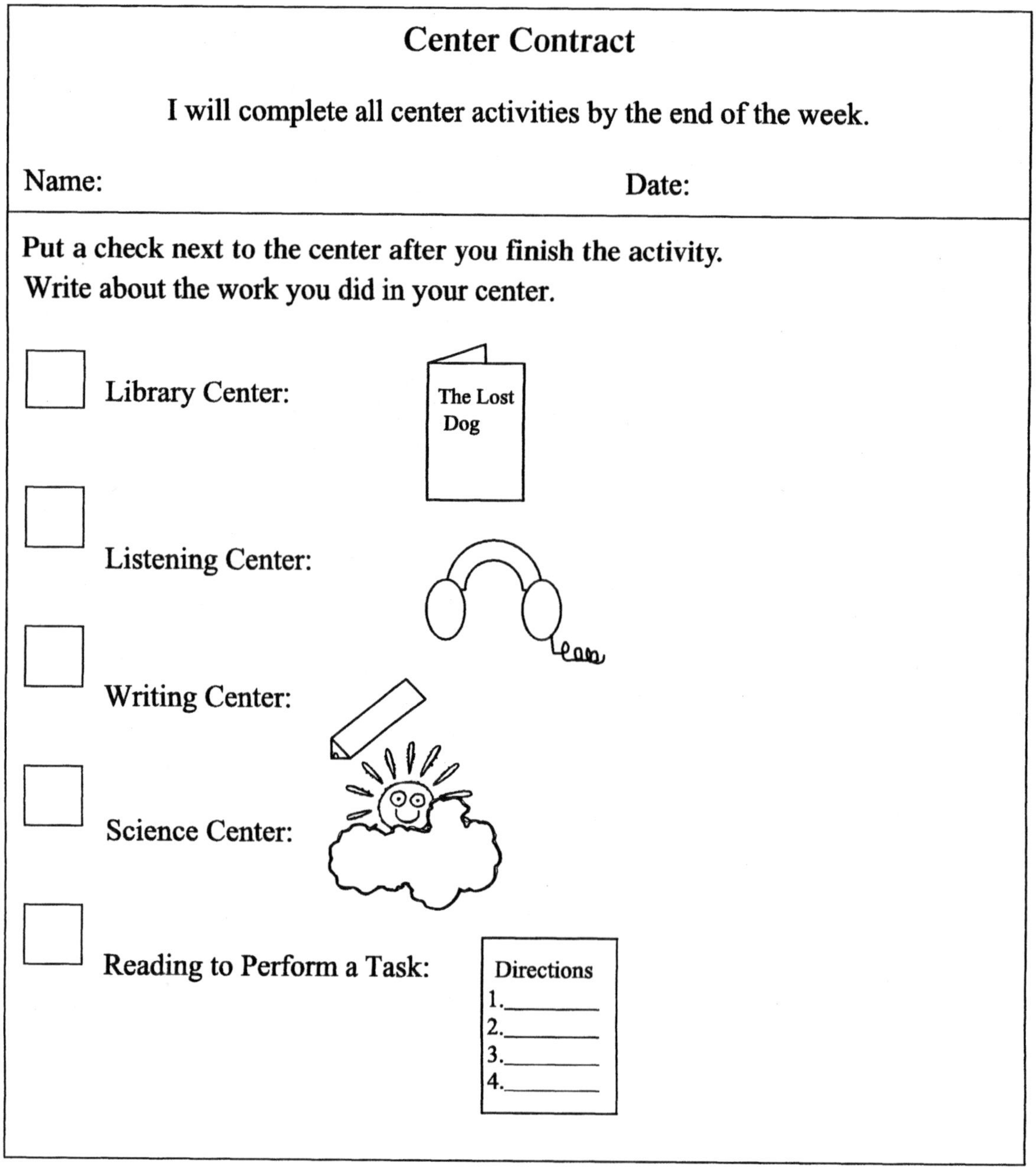

Center Contract

I will complete all center activities by the end of the week.

Name: Date:

Put a check next to the center after you finish the activity.
Write about the work you did in your center.

☐ Library Center:

☐ Listening Center:

☐ Writing Center:

☐ Science Center:

☐ Reading to Perform a Task:

Assigned Center Chart

If you are a teacher who needs to be in control of your students while they attend centers due to student behavior issues or your own behavior management style, then the best option for your class would be an assigned center chart. To create an assigned center chart:

1. Purchase a large pocket chart.

2. Use sentence strips to write the center assignments.

3. Use color index cards to create student name cards. Students that are in the same reading group should have the same color name cards.

4. Place the student name cards vertically behind the assigned center card so their name can be seen above the center they have been assigned to. Only two students from each group or of the same color name cards can be placed behind each center assignment at a time.

Figure 9.8
Assigned Center Chart

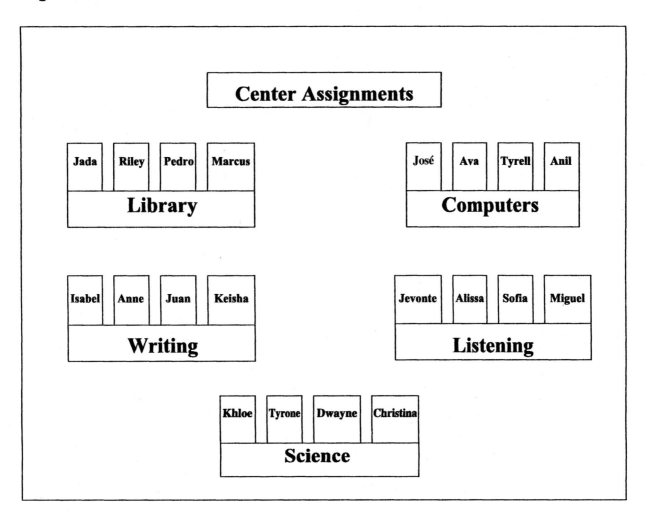

Seatwork Assignments

Seatwork is one of the work areas that students will rotate to during the reading group rotations. Seatwork can be implemented many different ways. Some teachers require students to complete a reading assignment and a comprehension or vocabulary words activity. Other teachers require students to complete a set of written instructions or seatwork steps (see figure 9.9). Seatwork steps can be written on the chalkboard, written on chart paper, or written on sentence strips and placed in a pocket chart. If necessary, provide picture clues for struggling readers to be able to complete the steps independently. It is the teacher's decision if the steps will be generic or change daily. Another option is to differentiate the seatwork steps according to reading group abilities by writing the steps on individual half sheets of paper.

Figure 9.9
Generic Example of Seatwork Steps

Seatwork Steps

Step #1   Complete your seatwork assignment.

Step #2   Complete today's word wall assignment.

Step #3   Read a book from the classroom library.

Step #4   Write in your journal.

Work Quietly!

Chapter 10
Helpful Hints about the Hidden Curriculum

As if cross-referencing the state and district curriculum weren't enough work, now you tell me there's a *hidden curriculum*. Well, where's it hiding?

The hidden curriculum consists of unwritten topics and lessons which should be taught, but are not required, in order to provide students with a well-rounded education.

Exposing the Hidden Curriculum

The hidden curriculum isn't taught in college or explained at a faculty meeting, it is just something that occurs naturally in a classroom sometimes without the teacher even realizing it. The following is a list of hidden curriculum examples:

- Teach the traditions for all of the celebrated holidays throughout the year.

- Use President's Day or Lincoln and Washington's birthdays to teach the history of past presidents.

- Teach good behaviors by integrating a lesson on sharing because maybe your class is not able to take turns politely.

- Answer inquisitive questions that arise or give a definition for and discuss an unfamiliar word that the class has encountered in a book.

- Teach students about the concept of *responsibility* by letting students take care of a class pet.

- Answer questions or explain concepts while on a field trip.

Teachable Moments

Spontaneous teachable moments can happen as you are teaching or while your class is out at recess. Teachable moments could also occur when a child has an intriguing question about the lesson topic or about something they have seen, heard, or just want to know more about. When you take a moment out of your lesson or schedule to teach something that wasn't planned for, that's a teachable moment. A day can be filled with teachable moments; for example, while standing in line for lunch a student asks his teacher, "How much money do I have?," and his teacher replies, "Well, you tell me. You have two dimes and they are each worth ten cents, how much do you have?" And the child exclaims, "Oh, ten plus ten, I have twenty cents!"

Morning Work Assignment Ideas

Who are we trying to kid—mornings are hectic and because of this the students need to be kept busy as you bustle about the classroom making last-minute preparations for the school day. Morning work is simply the assignment or task that the students must complete after they enter the classroom in the morning and before announcements begin. Morning work ideas could be to:

- complete a journal entry on any given topic.

- complete a journal entry on an assigned topic or from a sentence starter.

- record the homework assignments.

- read a book of choice.

- complete an activity worksheet.

- play a board game with a partner.

- work on completing a puzzle.

- complete a task by following written directions.

- complete work from a lesson given the previous day.

- attend a center.

The Morning News

The morning news develops the student's oral language and offers many avenues for writing teaching points. Writing the morning news is a great way for the teacher to model writing fluency and demonstrate writing skills. The morning news can be differentiated to meet the needs of both primary and intermediate grades.

Primary Morning News

In the primary grades, the morning news can offer many mini lesson opportunities on writing, such as matching print to speech, stretch spelling words with students, demonstrating letter and word formations, modeling fluent writing, spacing between words, capital letters, usage of words, spelling, punctuation marks, complete sentences, and oral language. The following are ideas for implementing the morning news in a primary classroom:

- Primary students usually meet as a group on the rug and write the morning news on a wipe board or chart paper.

- The morning news is written by the teacher as volunteers for the morning news dictate a title and facts or news events about the day. Each sentence should be written with a different color marker to help struggling readers see where one sentence ends and another begins.

- A volunteer should be challenged to create a title for the morning news that begins with the same sound that the day of the week does, such as Monkey Monday Morning News or Math Monday Morning News.

- Choose a few volunteers to dictate facts about the day. The dictation should be written like so:

Monkey Monday Morning News

Isabel said, "Today we are learning about graphs in math."

Tyrell said, "We will paint in art class today."

Dominic said, "It is cold and windy outside."

- Volunteers could also help write words, sentences, or punctuation marks in order to participate in the writing experience.

- Reread the morning news aloud and track the words with a pointer as you read with the students.

- Ask two or three more volunteers to interact with the morning news through the use of sticky notes or markers in order to identify or highlight one of the following:

    — A capital or lower case letter.

    — A word or part of a word they know.

    — Spelling.

    — A punctuation mark, comma, or quotation marks.

    — A noun, pronoun, verb, adjective, or compound word.

    — How many words they can count within a sentence.

Intermediate Morning News

The intermediate morning news is an oral language experience which gives students independent or group practice with proofreading, correction marks, capitalization, usage of words, punctuation, and spelling. The following are ideas for implementing the morning news in the intermediate classroom:

- Intermediate students usually sit at their desk as the morning news is written or displayed on the chalkboard, overhead projector, or chart paper.

- The intermediate morning news could be prewritten with mistakes or with words purposely left out by the teacher in order to challenge the students to try rewriting the news correctly in their journals. Another option is to allow volunteers to use correction marks directly on the morning news in order to identify the mistakes found.

- Intermediate morning news could be a morning work activity that is completed before announcements and checked after announcements.

<u>our morning news</u>

we wll exchange lbry boks tody

it is sofias birthday tody.

we are haveing Fish sticks and piza for lnch

Calendar Time

Calendar time is basically an interactive drill or review of math concepts. Calendar activities can be done with the whole group congregating at the carpet area. Calendar activities could be completed in the morning, after lunch, after recess, before math, or after math depending on your scheduling needs. The activity and display ideas below will help you create and use your calendar area:

- Identify and recite the months of the year in order.

- Identify and write the date: Today is *(month) (date), (year)*.

- Continue and label a pattern.

- A hundreds chart for rote counting numbers up to 100 or practice skip counting.

- Track how many days we've been in school with tally marks or by adding straws to a ones, tens, hundreds chart.

- Display money amounts within a pocket chart using coins which match the equivalence to the amount of days students have been in school (for 95 days show 95 cents).

- Display a monthly math poem that matches the concept that you are currently teaching from the math curriculum to choral read with the students on a daily basis.

- Compare small, medium, and large by ordering objects by descending size in a pocket chart.

- Identify the daily weather by representing it on a graph or weather wheel.

Spelling

Most schools do not have a curriculum guide to help their teacher's plan for spelling. If a spelling guide is not available, then it is teacher's discretion which words will be studied, how many words will be assigned, when the words will be practiced, and how the words will be practiced. To help with all of these spelling choices, see the tips below:

- Spelling tests can begin as early as January of the student's first grade year.

- First and second grade students should receive three to five words per week; any more may be overwhelming for their age group.

- Third through fifth grade students can receive up to ten words per week.

- Words can be chosen from a grade-level word list, an anthology, or a reading book.

- Make spelling meaningful by choosing words with repetitive spelling patterns; for example, right, night, fight, light, bright. Practicing spelling patterns will benefit student reading abilities.

- Differentiate the spelling words according to the student's reading group or abilities.

- Give a bonus word for students who need to be challenged.

- Revisit spelling words by having a mixed review at the end of the month that includes words from previous spelling patterns.

- Record the student's spelling progress in your grade book or data binder. This could be done by creating a spread sheet on your word processor that lists the student names, spelling words or spelling patterns assigned, and a grade reflecting whether or not they mastered each spelling word or spelling pattern.

- Assign spelling work that will motivate students to practice their spelling words, such as:

  — Rainbow Writing: writing the word once in pencil then tracing over it five more times with a different color crayon each time.

  — Generate a crossword puzzle or word search with the spelling words.

  — Have students match the spelling words to pictures or require them to illustrate the words.

  — Motivate students to use the spelling words to write a silly short story.

— Scramble the spelling words and challenge student to unscramble them.

— Play the game Word Detective by giving students clues that describe a mystery spelling word and they must use the clue to figure out which word is being described and then write the word.

— Allow students to keep a spelling journal. The spelling journal can be used for word practice and as a reference during writing assignments.

— Illustrate each spelling word and write the spelling word inside of the illustration. Direct the students to repetitively write the word around the perimeter of the picture until the entire perimeter has been covered.

— Introduce Pyramid, which is a fun way for students to practice writing their spelling words. See examples below:

c	f	p
ca	fr	pa
car	fri	pas
carv	frie	past
carve	frien	paste
carved	friend	pastel

Writing

Providing many opportunities for writing experiences will improve your students' writing skills. Writing can often become tedious or boring to students if the only writing experience they are exposed to is that of the scheduled writing block. During the writing block students watch the teacher model a writing piece, students write a rough draft, edit and revise their rough draft (sometimes twice), write a final copy, and then they meet with the teacher to discuss their final product.

While understanding and completing the writing process is important, it is also exhausting for some children. Revive your student's perspective on writing by providing writing experiences such as:

● Give students random pictures from a magazine and ask them to write about what they see or have them make up an interesting story about the picture.

● Pass out story starters or the beginning to a funny or kooky story and have students use their imagination to write the middle and end events.

● Integrate science and social studies into the writing block by allowing students to reflect on what they have learned from those lesson activities through writing and illustrating.

- Make stamps available with a variety of pictures so students can write a rebus story. A rebus story contains sentences that incorporate both pictures and words to tell events.

- Allow students to write friendly letters to one another or to pen pals from other classes.

- Explain to the students how to *write the room*. In order to write the room, students will need a clipboard or a spiral notebook, a writing tool (pencil, pen, or marker), and paper. As the student walks around with these items, they write and illustrate words they can read that are displayed around the room.

- Provide each student with a journal so they may reflect on topics freely through writing and drawing.

- Let students work independently or in cooperative groups to make or write books.

- Establish a paper station where students can access construction paper, stationery, lined paper, envelopes, cards, or stickers to use for writing activities.

- Use the computer lab in order to give students the opportunity to type poems and short stories that they have previously written.

Recess

The playground offers endless possibilities for teachable moments. By observing your students' interactions, you will find out a lot about their personal interests, social skills, compassion, attitudes, and gross motor skill capabilities. If you utilize your recess time to observe student interactions, you will probably agree that recess is just as important to students as reading, writing, and math. To get the most out of recess, pick through these tips:

- Carry a whistle and keep sunglasses handy so that students can hear you and you can see them at all times.

- Establish playground rules and boundaries that students must not go beyond.

- Keep a first aid kit and nurse passes with you at all times.

- Organize team-building activities such as jump rope or kickball.

- Monitor student social interactions and hold brief discussions with students who are being disrespectful to others.

- Try to get the loner student to mingle with the rest of the group and help them to build on their social skills.

- Create friendships by matching two students together who look bored or lonely.

- Bring in balls (soft ones), jump ropes, Frisbees, and sidewalk chalk for students to entertain themselves with.

- Do not condone injury-prone recess activities such as tag, dodge ball, or football.

The Class Pet

A class pet is a wonderful way to teach students about responsibility and the basic needs of living things. Although a class pet might sound fun, it can quickly turn into a nightmare from the teacher's perspective if a few do's and don'ts are not considered. For instance:

Class Pet Do's

- Ask your principal's permission to be able to keep a class pet.

- Assign students to care for the pet.

- Make sure that a class pet is a responsibility that you truly want to add to your classroom. A class plant is just as fun for students to take care of.

- Choose a safe pet that can't hurt the students by biting or pinching, such as a fish, lizard, frog, or ant farm.

Class Pet Don'ts

- Don't purchase turtles. Turtles can carry diseases such as salmonella.

- Don't purchase animals with hair. Animals such as guinea pigs, rabbits, and hamsters can carry dander in their fur and can cause an allergic reaction for a lot of students (not to mention, animals with hair typically bite).

- Don't purchase a pet that requires a lot of upkeep. Remember, your time is valuable.

★**Tip:** A class pet alternative for the primary grades is to place a stuffed animal (a dog, cat, or rabbit) in a small pet tote. Inside the pet tote also include books on animal care or fictitious books about the type of animal you have chosen and a composition notebook. Each night a different student can take the class pet home with them, read the books included in the pet tote, and write about their time spent with the class pet in the composition notebook. Another class pet alternative for either primary or intermediate grades is to purchase a lifelike fish aquarium that contains plastic fish. There is virtually no upkeep and kids love it!

Field Trips

Field trips merge classroom learning with the real-world experience. A field trip is a wonderful way to build on a child's background knowledge or experiences, but there is a lot of paperwork, planning, and responsibility that come with this adventure. Let's get those wheels on the bus going round and round for your field trip. Here are some helpful field trip practices:

- Field trips are usually taken once per quarter or twice a year, depending on the school and grade level's decision.

- Field trips to the really popular sights fill up fast and should be booked the previous school year, in the summer, or very early in the new school year.

- Field trips that are booked must connect to the curriculum and support learning that has recently occurred in class or before the learning that will take place in order to build student background knowledge. Sometimes the order in which you teach the units in your curriculum will need to be switched around in order to match your lessons to the scheduled field trip date.

- How to plan for a field trip:

  — Discuss field trip ideas during grade-level meetings.

  — Book the field trip as soon as possible.

  — Fill out the paperwork required by your school and wait on an approval. If it is not approved, simply cancel the tentative date scheduled with the field trip site coordinator.

  — Find out how many people will attend the trip, including students, teachers, and chaperones. Once you have established how many will be attending, tentatively reserve a bus with a bus company that your school already does business with. Your school secretary will give you this information or book the bus for you.

  — Become familiar with the field trip site, the contact person, the expected method of payment, and the site's rules and regulations. Request an information packet from the field trip site in order to do so.

  — After the trip is approved by administrators, send out the field trip permission slip forms three weeks in advance. This will give the parents time to send in the necessary money amount.

- As the field trip date approaches, tie up these loose ends:

  — Call the field trip site to confirm reservations and last-minute details or questions.

  — Create an itinerary for the field trip that gives times, information on when students will depart from school, the estimated destination arrival time, how the group will check in, scheduled activities, the time scheduled for lunch and the lunch procedures, what time to meet back at the bus, and the estimated time for arrival back at the school.

— Put together a chaperone packet that includes the itinerary, your cell phone number (in case of an emergency), a list of student names that make up the group they will chaperone, a map of the field trip site, and any other important information.

— Inform the nurse one week in advance of your scheduled field trip so the nurse can give the teachers on your grade level their student's medications.

— Choose your chaperones and as early as possible inform your chaperones that they have been chosen so they can take off from work. In your letter to the chaperones state how grateful you are that they could participate, what to bring (a watch, lunch, cell phone, and a tote bag to carry their groups lunches in), what time to meet at the school, the field trip rules for the children, guidelines for the chaperones (do not buy souvenirs or food for the students since it is unfair to others, please be prompt when arriving in the morning, be prompt for departure from the field trip site).

— Inform the school secretary a week in advance so she can prepare the necessary checks for the bus company and field trip site.

— Make name tags for students to wear during the field trip with the school name, school address, and school phone number.

— Develop a follow-up activity for students to be able to reflect on what they have learned while on their field trip once they arrive back to school.

- The day before the field trip:

  — Send a reminder notice home to parents telling them to send in a bagged lunch (no glass bottles), dress their child appropriately in clothing for the weather, wear tennis shoes, if necessary put on sunscreen, bring a hat, and refrain from sending in any money since we will not be going into the souvenir shops.

  — Assign groups for your chaperones and keep a list of the groups for yourself.

- The day of the field trip:

  — Dress appropriately for the field trip in comfortable walking shoes and clothes.

  — Pack a lunch for yourself.

  — Get the checks from the secretary for the bus company and the field trip site.

  — Remember to get a receipt for both checks and give them to the secretary at the end of the field trip.

— Fill your tote bag with the class roster, student emergency cards, student medications, a first aid kit, a camera, your cell phone, and your lunch.

— Be sure that all chaperone forms have been signed and distribute the chaperone packets of information. Don't forget to include the following information on your chaperone packets: your cell phone number in case of emergencies and a list of student names that are in the group the chaperone is responsible for.

— Place name tags on your students and tell them to keep them on all day for safety reasons.

— Instruct students to give their lunches to the chaperones and to use the restroom before departure.

— Call roll before the bus departs to go to and from the field trip site. All students must be accounted for.

— After arriving back at school, discuss the events of the day and then distribute and explain the follow-up activity.

Helping Students Cope with Loss

One of the most heart-wrenching ordeals that a teacher will encounter will be helping students cope with loss. Any type of change in a child's life can be devastating, so when they are faced with losing someone close to them, losing their house by means of disaster or financial issues, or losing through divorce what they have always known to be their family unit, they will turn to their teacher and school for comfort. Without even realizing it, the teacher provides comfort for all of the students on a daily basis through their caring smile, words of encouragement, scheduled routine, and safe environment where students know they will never be hurt or left hungry. No matter what happens in the student's life, they can count on you to be there. The following ideas will help the teacher provide support for those students who are coping with a loss:

● Make every effort to keep the student in good spirits.

● Give the student a secure feeling by staying consistent with your scheduled routines.

● Give the student an item of interest to take home with them so that they can be reminded of their security at school.

● Provide books on the topic that the student is dealing with that have characters they can connect and relate their lives to. This will help the student understand that they are not alone or the only ones who have ever faced this type of loss.

- Schedule meeting times for the guidance counselor to work with the student. The guidance counselor is trained in grief therapy and it gives the student a chance to discuss their emotions in a private setting.

- Communicate with the parents so that everyone is updated on the student's emotional progress.

- Let the student bring in something special such as a picture or toy that has sentimental value and helps the student feel secure.

- Encourage the student to play during recess by generating a class kickball game or organizing an activity that includes the student who needs a little extra attention and a small group of sympathetic students.

- Give the student a special journal or diary so they can write or draw about their feelings at any given time.

- Tell the student that you care and that you are there if they need someone to talk to but don't overstate this if the child seems to be doing better by not talking about it for the time being.

- If the child has lost a friend or family member, assist them with creating a memory box that can be decorated by hot gluing special pictures and other decorative items to the outside of the box. Then instruct the student to fill the box with memories of their lost loved one and to visit the contents of the box when they would like to remember the good times they were able to share with that special someone.

- You could help a child and his or her family rebuild their lives when their home is struck by disaster through collecting home items donated by students and colleagues.

Chapter 11
Useful Graphic Organizers

Graphic organizers are convenient and easy to use as formative assessments that can be applied across the curriculum to organize important information. *Tip: All of the following graphic organizers can be enlarged to poster size and laminated for use over and over or made larger than life by drawing them on plain color sheets or plastic tablecloths in order to use for group activities. The following graphic organizers are explained below and provided as black line masters for your teaching convenience:

T-Chart

The *T-Chart* (figure 11.1) is utilized in order to compare two items to see how they are the same and/or different. Item ideas which could be compared are:

- Objects
- Places
- Stories
- Living Things
- Non-Living Things

Sequence Chain

The *Sequence Chain* (figure 11.2) requires students to put events in order. Ideas for events which could be sequenced:

- Story Events
- Daily Events
- Historical Events
- Life Cycles

Story Pie

The *Story Pie* (figure 11.3) is used to draw and/or write story events in order. Each event is drawn sequentially within a slice or section of the pie until the pie is full. The teacher should decide ahead of time how many slices the pie will contain based on the number of events that need to be recorded.

Venn Diagram

A *Venn Diagram* (figure 11.4) compares two items to see how they are different (represented in the opposite sides of the squares) and alike (the center of the square where they meet). Item ideas for comparing likenesses and differences could be:

- Living Things
- Non-Living Things
- Stories
- Places

KWL Chart

The *KWL Chart* (figure 11.5) is used for recording (either by the teacher, students, or both) what students know, want to know, and have learned about a topic. The *Know* and *Want to Know* section of the chart should be completed before the learning of the topic occurs, like a warm-up, and doing so gives the teacher insight about the student's background knowledge. The *Learned* section of the *KWL Chart* should be completed after the learning of the topic has occurred. ★**Tip:** If the teacher is recording student responses, be sure to use different color markers for each response and label each with the name of the student who gave the response.

Idea Web

An *Idea Web* (figure 11.6) is an organizer which can be used to record facts on a topic or the student's knowledge and/or ideas, which is typically called brainstorming. The topic is usually placed in the center of the web and the information on the topic is recorded as branches off of the given topic.

Main Idea Table

The *Main Idea Table* (figure 11.7) is shaped like a table because the *tabletop* displays the main topic and the *legs* of the table display the details which support the main idea.

Decision Tree

The *Decision Tree* (figure 11.8) is used to organize thoughts and ideas of students in reference to personal life decisions which they must weigh the pros and cons for. The *Decision Tree* could also be used to make inferences on decisions that characters could weigh in stories based on what they have read.

Story Map

The *Story Map* (figure 11.9) is a comprehension organizer that provides space for the student to record the who, what, when, where, why, and how components of a story.

Effect/Cause Chart

The *Effect and Cause Chart* (figure 11.10) is used to record exactly that. List the effect first and the cause second, since it is easier for students to comprehend the concept when explained like so: "The effect is what happens because of something causing it to happen." Students could be required to fill out both the effect and cause section of the chart or just one or the other—the effect or cause—depending on the learning expectations.

Beginning, Middle, and End Events Chart

The *Beginning, Middle, and End Events Chart* (figure 11.11) provides an organized method for recording the main events within:

- Stories

- Daily Routines

- Historical Events

Problem/Solution Chart

The *Problem / Solution Chart* (figure 11.12) is an organized way for students to record the problem or situation that went wrong and how the possible solution or how the problem was solved. The problem solution chart can be used for reflecting on:

- Story Events

- Personal Problems

- Character Dilemmas

Figure 11.1

T-Chart

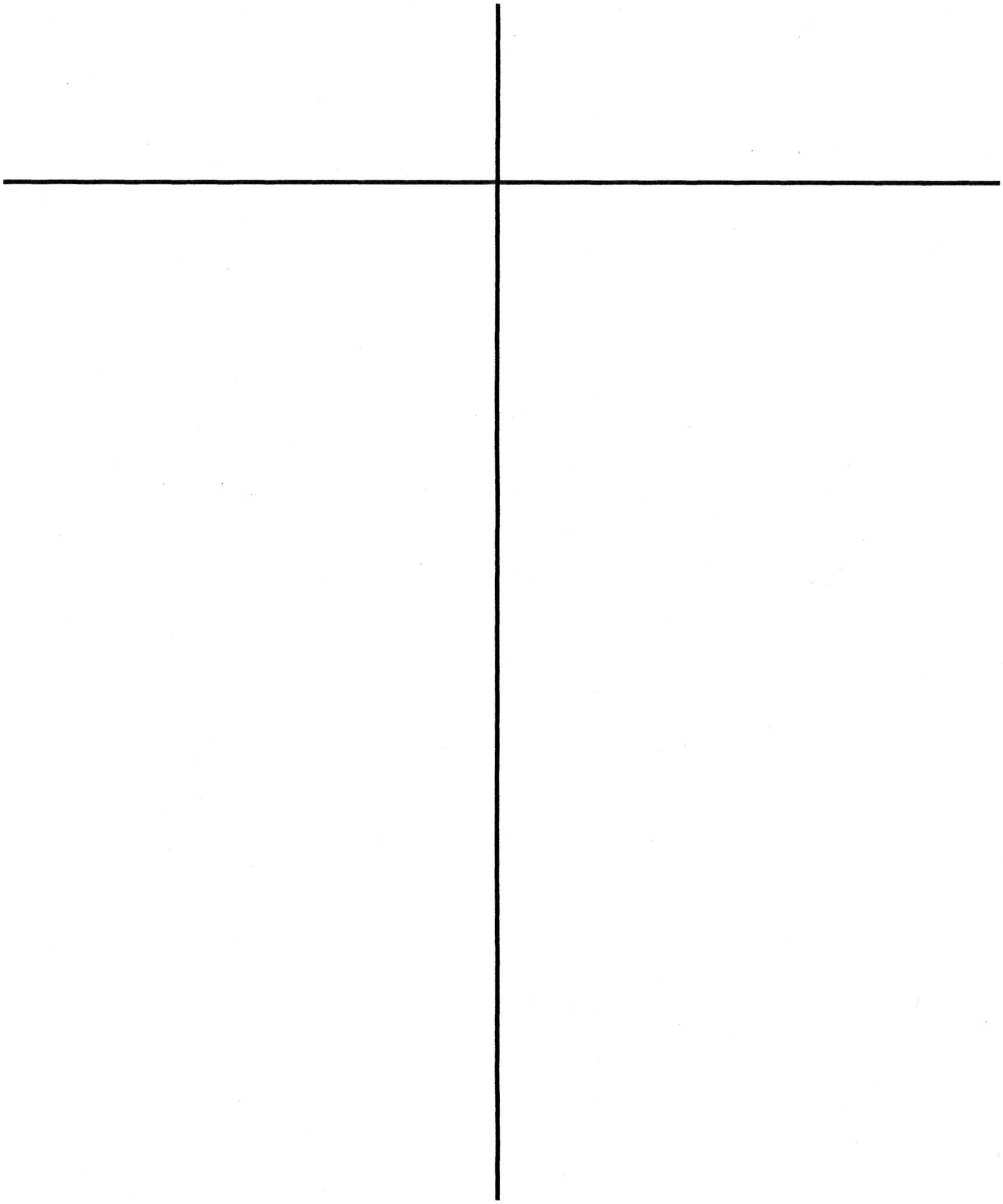

Figure 11.2

Sequence Chain

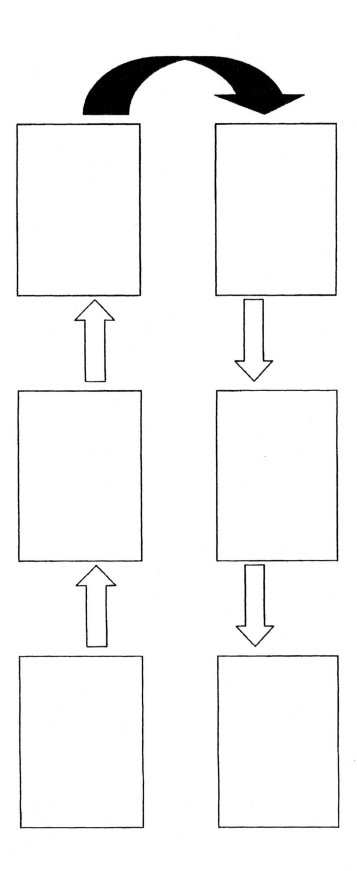

Figure 11.3

Story Pie

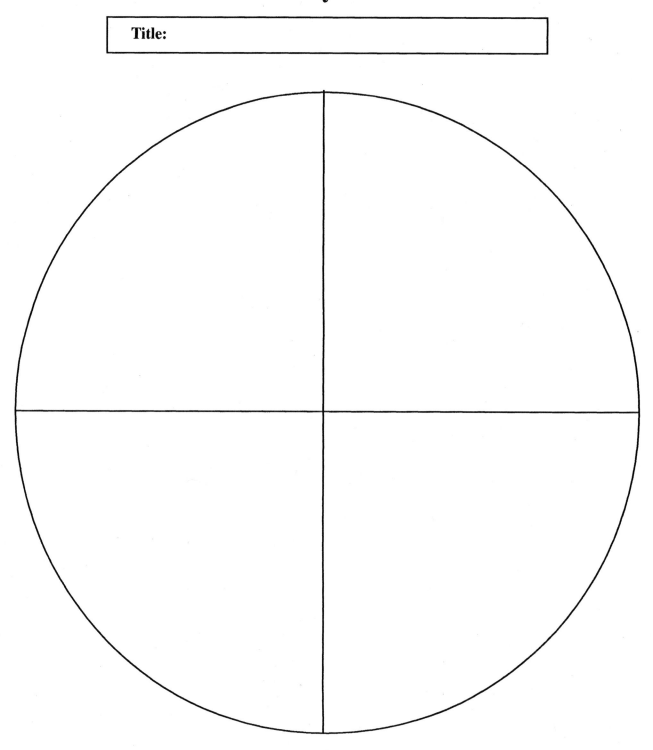

Figure 11.4

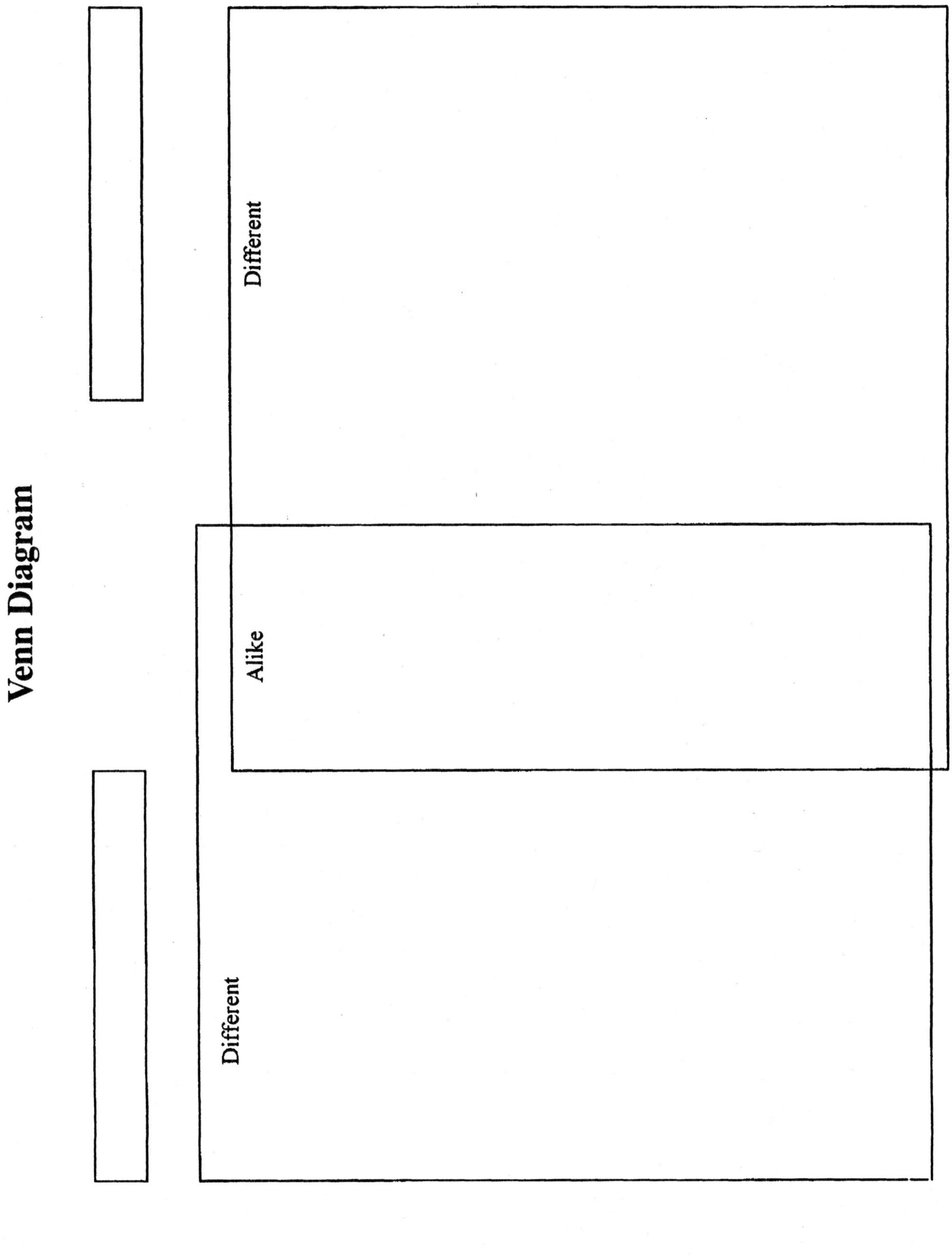

Venn Diagram

Different

Alike

Different

Figure 11.5

KWL Chart

K	W	L
What do you know?	What do you want to know?	What did you learn?

Figure 11.6

Idea Web

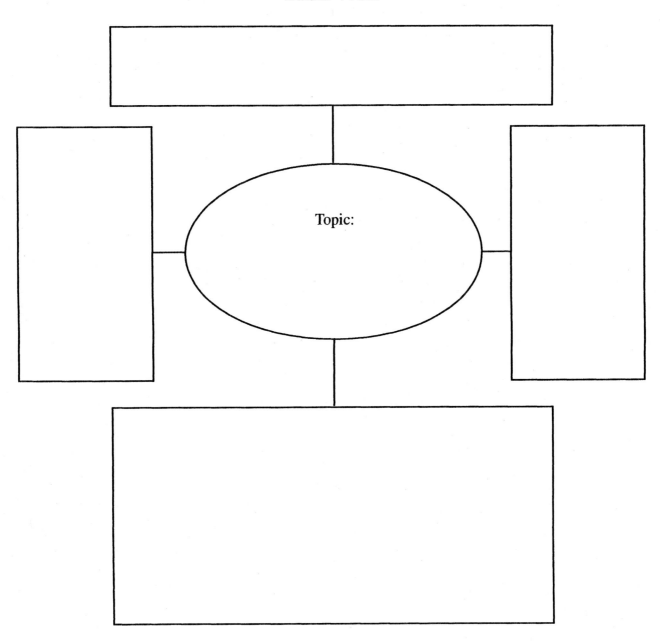

Figure 11.7

Main Idea Table

Main Idea:

Supporting Detail

Supporting Detail

Supporting Detail

Supporting Detail

Figure 11.8

The Decision Tree

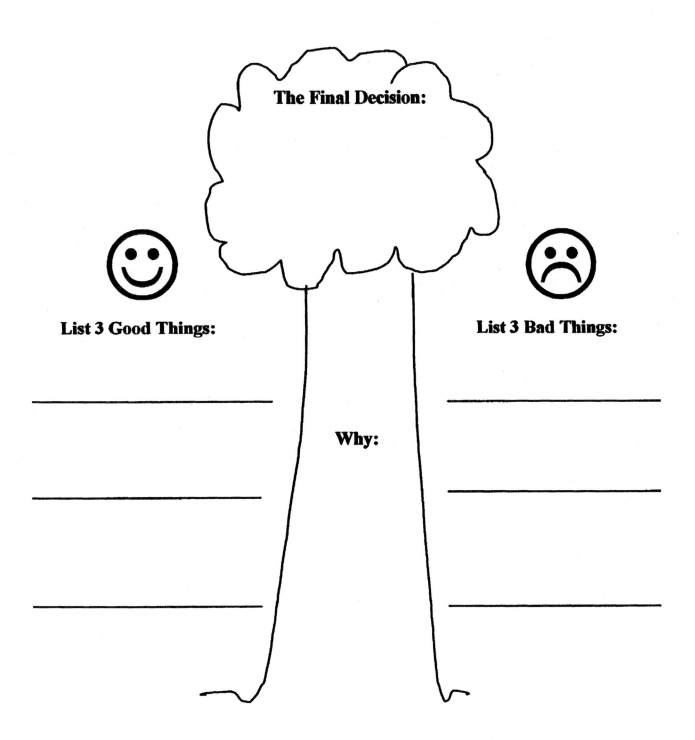

Figure 11.9

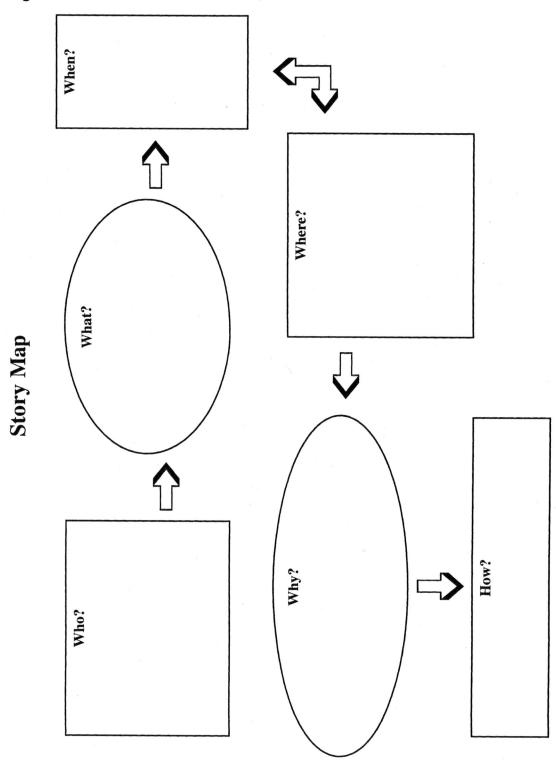

Story Map

Figure 11.10

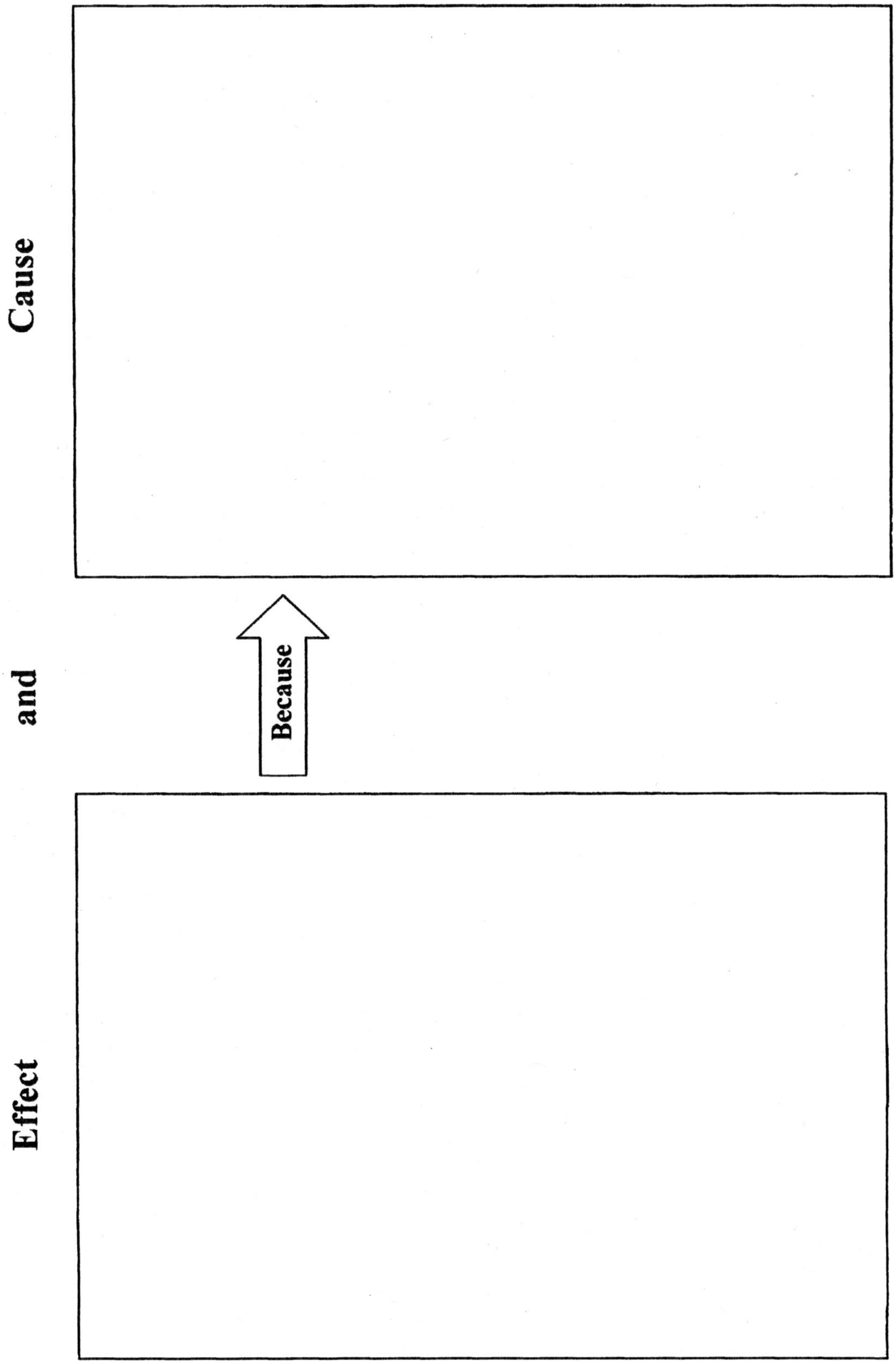

Cause

and

Effect

Because

Figure 11.11

Identify the Beginning, Middle, and End Events

In the beginning of the story .

In the middle....

At the end of the story ..

Figure 11.12

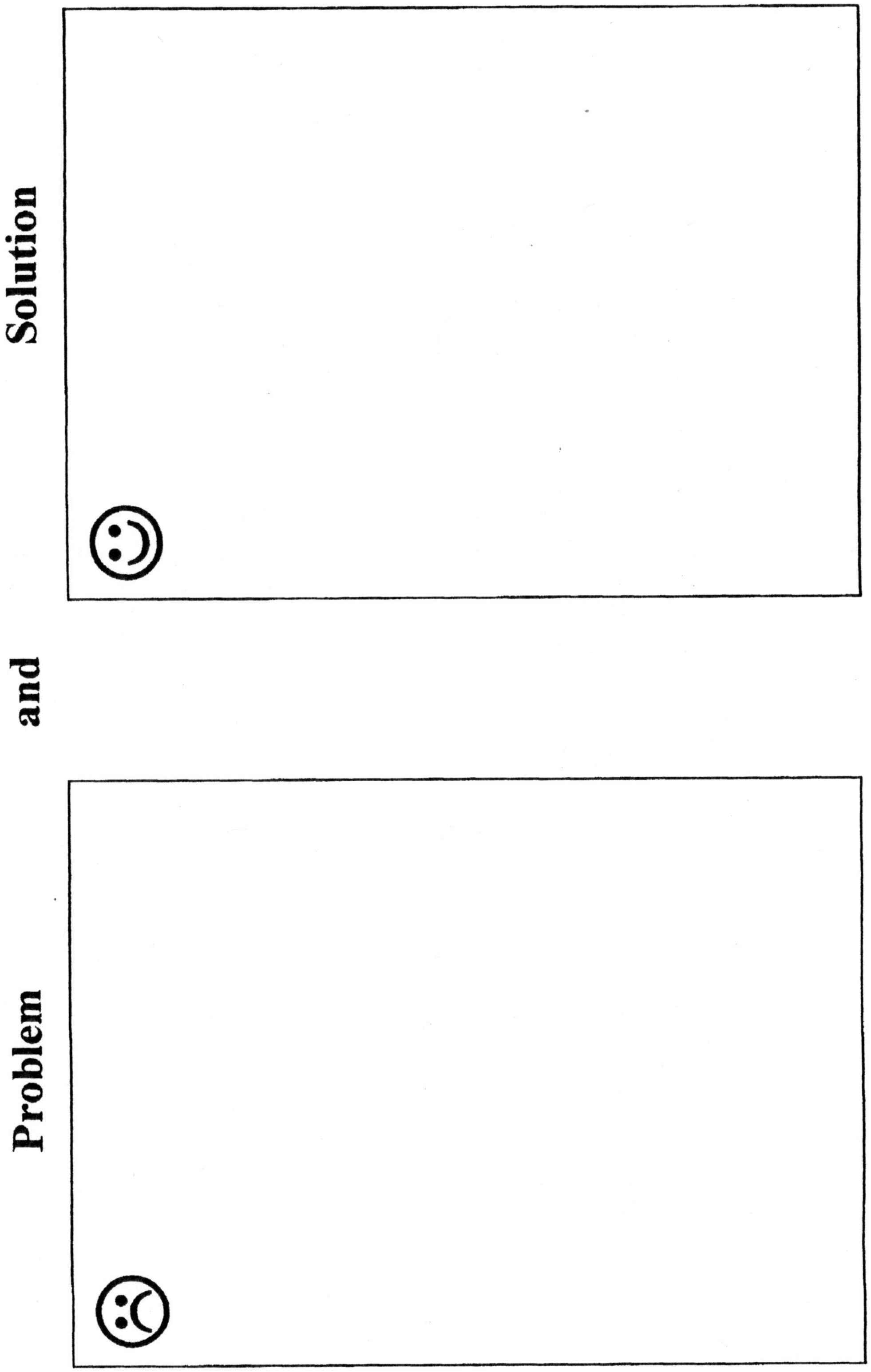

Solution

and

Problem

Closing Thoughts

It takes a special person to be a teacher and not just anyone can fulfill the job requirements. Teaching is a demanding career which requires compassion, patience, perseverance, flexibility, and the ability to multitask and think swiftly on your feet. Although teaching is demanding, it is also a fun and very rewarding career that has a title which people generally respect.

The keys to success for establishing a happy marriage between you and your teaching career are simple. You must form good work habits and know your limits. Ways to avoid *burning-out* are:

- Walk, don't run… pacing can prove very beneficial in all that you do.

- Communicate your feelings. Don't be afraid to say *no* to taking on tasks that you don't have time or sanity for. If you have trouble saying the word *no* to others, then try saying this instead: "Thanks for having faith in me but I don't feel as if I can handle that responsibility right now."

- Realize that you are your worst critic and don't be too hard on yourself. Remember that there is no such thing as *perfect*. Too much of your precious time can be exhausted if you continue to perfect something that is fine just the way it already is.

- Know that you are unique, and with that uniqueness you will teach using methods that are best for you and your students, so never compare yourself to the teacher next door. There are 101 ways to teach the same objective, so find the way that is best for you and your group of students.

- Never forget why you became a teacher and cling to that thought when you feel as if your boat is sinking. And if you are sure that your boat has sunk, don't give up hope—call out for a life preserver. Your colleagues and administrators can be a valuable resource if you go to them for help or advice. Remember, you are never alone, and what better company to have than another compassionate teacher.

- Tough it out; nothing good comes easy. If you stay in the teaching profession you will make a positive impact on the future. Six hundred to over one thousand students could pass through your classroom door and look up to you as their mentor whom they expect will build their knowledge and character so that they may become a well-rounded citizen that will hopefully one day serve a positive, purposeful function in our society (no pressure or anything).

- Most of all, enjoy your students and take pride in their success, because their success is your success!

Index

Selected Resources

Clay, Marie. (2000). Running records for classroom teachers. Auckland, NZ: Heinemann Primary.

Dolch, E. (2003). Dolch sight word activities volumes 1&2. Columbus, OH: School Specialty Publishing.

Kujawa, S. & Huske, L. (1995). Strategic teaching and reading project: Updated edition. North Central Regional Educational Laboratory.

About the Author

Belinda Christine Tetteris is a Baltimore County public school teacher for the state of Maryland with many years of teaching experience in elementary education for both urban and rural school districts. Receiving her education from the College of Notre Dame of Maryland, she earned a dual Bachelor of Arts Cum Laude degree in both Elementary and Early Childhood and a dual Master of Arts degree in Leadership in Teaching and Reading. The Phi Xi chapter of the international honor society in education, Kappa Delta Pi, has recognized and awarded her outstanding contributions to education.